EVERY EVENING COMES THE MOON

AWAKENING THROUGH THE DARKNESS
OF THE SEPARATE SELF

BRIAN THERIAULT

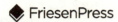

FriesenPress

One Printers Way
Altona, MB R0G 0B0
Canada

www.friesenpress.com

Copyright © 2022 by Brian Theriault, MEd, SEP, CCC
First Edition — 2022

This book is designed to provide helpful information. It is not intended as a substitute for psychological advice and treatment. The reader should consult with their physician in matters related to their mental wellness and particularly with respect to any symptoms that may require diagnosis or medical attention. Neither the publisher nor the author are responsible for any specific medical or psychological health needs that may require medical or psychological supervision and are not liable for any damages or negative consequences from any treatment, action, application or preparation to any person reading or following the information in this book.

All rights reserved.

No part of this publication may be reproduced in any form, or by any means, electronic or mechanical, including photocopying, recording, or any information browsing, storage, or retrieval system, without permission in writing from FriesenPress.

ISBN
978-1-03-913633-5 (Hardcover)
978-1-03-913632-8 (Paperback)
978-1-03-913634-2 (eBook)

1. BODY, MIND & SPIRIT, INSPIRATION & PERSONAL GROWTH

Distributed to the trade by The Ingram Book Company

EVERY EVENING COMES THE MOON

AWAKENING THROUGH THE DARKNESS
OF THE SEPARATE SELF

Dedication

This book is dedicated to my beautiful wife, Nadine Nowatzki, who passed away in 2015, and who mirrored the gifts of love and grace in the presence of death to me. In the darkest depths of human consciousness, you revealed the moonlight of awareness. I am eternally grateful to you. I love you deeply.

In Loving Gratitude

To Gary Tzu, a heartfelt, wild man who reflected my true nature back to me.

To my dearest friend Marcia Rich, a dancer within the mandala of existence who showed me how to see what has yet to be revealed.

To Lao Tzu, Osho, A.H. Almaas, and the many mystics and spiritual teachers who have helped me lose my footing along the way.

To Kathy, my Lilith, my Kali, my partner in sacred union.

To my editor, Jeannine Bourrier, who skillfully brought these words to life.

To my friends and family who supported me throughout this journey.

To the transcendent beauty of Nelson, British Columbia, Canada, where the majority of this book was written.

And especially to the many people I have had the opportunity to work with therapeutically. Your fearlessness in diving into the nondual journey and trusting the unfolding process is a rare gift indeed.

A Note About the Book

The journey of awakening is filled with paradox, and this book is an attempt to point to *that* which cannot be described. The concepts of "enlightenment," "nondual awakening," "truth," "wholeness," "Christ consciousness," "awakening," "self- realization," "consciousness," "emptiness," "the void," "stillness," "silence," and the like, are used interchangeably to point to the awakened stateless state of our true nature. This is done intentionally as a means of evoking a possible resonance within the reader as to what is being discussed throughout the book. The book is also comprised of personal anecdotes, stories, and interviews I have conducted over the years and when completing my master's thesis on the nondual journey of awakening, as well as clinical case studies and personal communications with colleagues and friends, to illustrate various aspects, dilemmas, and experiences found along the journey. Pseudonyms have been used where appropriate to ensure anonymity. Waking up to who and what we are as human beings does not follow a specific process. I have, nonetheless, grouped a collection of commonly found experiences throughout the nondual path as a series that makes sense for the reader.

An Invitation from the Author

Right now, in this very moment, you are complete and whole just as you are. There is absolutely nothing wrong with you, despite whatever you may think, feel, or even experience. Who you are in this very instant is completely perfect. And yet, for the majority of us, this inherent wholeness we have always ever been has apparently been lost, resulting in an endless search to recover it. The problem is we believe wholeness exists outside ourselves in some future moment in time and some particular experience. This is the birth of the seeker; the little self, the "me," the "I," who we think we are, seeking wholeness, awakening, and enlightenment or whatever we want to call it, in persons, places, things, and experiences – even spiritual experiences. At a deep level, we are all seeking wholeness, whether it's through relationships, work, the bottle, or spiritual teachings, due to a deeply held belief that who and what "I am" is incomplete and somehow lacking in a fundamental way, which we desperately seek to avoid or attempt to cover up. But here's the thing, and at some level, you've probably already noticed it; the new relationship, the next bottle, the new career, and the new guru are all temporary aids to our sense of incompleteness and sense of lack. And when they begin to lose their ability to mask this lack we feel at the core of our being and give us the experience of wholeness we so desperately crave, we fall right back into the seeking game again, and hoping again, and again, that the next experience or relationship will somehow deliver us. We are nothing more than seeking junkies caught in a vicious loop because we are seeking *that* which we already are.

This book is an invitation to awaken to our inherent wholeness right in this very moment, no matter what we are experiencing, feeling, or believing about ourselves. It is an invitation to realize who and what we truly are and to jump out of the vicious loop of seeking wholeness, to realizing wholeness now in the midst of our present experience. It is waking up out of the dream of the seeker (the little self) and see *that* which is alive and whole right now, *this moment*, this very instant. And lastly, it is an offer to wake up to the wholeness that you are in this present moment, which is beyond any story you can ever tell yourself and beyond the experience of pain and pleasure, life and death, and space and time. Awakening to wholeness is seeing that this moment, as it is now, is entirely perfect, no matter what the experience is. There is no need to seek this, understand this, experience this, or even awaken to it – who you, we, and I truly are, is always already awake and alive right now and beyond any experience and understanding itself. In seeing this, we are whole. And to live from this realization is to live a life of fearless intensity and loving compassion.

Many people are waking up to this realization in everyday life. Many people are beginning to see through the dream of the separate self and realize what is real. But here's the rub, and this is what interests me the most; to realize the essence of who we are is one thing, but to live it in everyday life is quite another thing altogether. The darkness I speak of and what I am pointing to is the exclusive belief in a solid separate self amongst other selves. The darkness is the belief in the veil of separateness. It is the absolute belief in "me" and in "I."

The veil of separation was my constant moment-to-moment experience. I lived a life of quiet misery, disconnected from everyone, and feeling heavy. I felt fragmented and lost, always struggling to find my place in the world, and trying to connect and be like others. Other people seemed to do it with ease, and I often wondered what was wrong with me. This reinforced the belief that there was something wrong with me and that I was incomplete and lacking, so I would tirelessly pursue connections, whether I wanted them or not or whether they were based on authenticity or not. But don't get me wrong, I met some wonderful friends later in high school and my college years, however, I still felt incomplete, lost, and fragmented. My close friendships did nothing to heal my feelings of incompleteness. The heaviness was pervasive. From here, I joined the ranks of spiritual seekers and involved myself in many transformational groups, practiced many meditations, studied various spiritual teachings, and attended many spiritual workshops and nondual *Satsangs* – a gathering of spiritual seekers in front of a spiritual teacher who provides spiritual discourses followed by a question-and-answer period. Even though all of them were saying the same thing, "You are that which you're seeking," albeit, in many different ways, the essence of the message was consistent. "You are complete just as you are," but I didn't want to hear it. I was still under my self-imposed spell of believing someone or something would do it for me; that someone would bring me to total completeness and peace. I wouldn't accept that I was already complete and *whole now*. It took me a long time to see I did not want to accept the possibility of Wholeness now because it would mean the end of my seeking and the end of me and who I thought I was. Over the years, it was starting to dawn on me that I had invested so much energy and resources to support the seeking game and the image I had constructed of myself being a spiritual seeker seeking awakening. It would take many failed attempts at seeking wholeness in experiences outside myself before I finally surrendered and dropped the game of seeking altogether. When I stopped trying to find wholeness, trying to be enlightened and free, and trying to become other than what I already am at this moment, a profound stateless state of relaxation emerged. There was no more tension-seeking, no more pressure to become or to be different from what I already am, and there was no need to defend myself. I could *just be*. This is it. Extraordinarily, as I grew older, I began to see and experience this realization in some of my most traumatizing and difficult moments. Even in the midst of pain, Wholeness existed. It completely changed the way I viewed myself and the world, and subsequently transformed my work as a therapist. The possibility of awakening existed in the therapeutic setting. Buddhist traditions refer to awakening as the "ultimate medicine" where healing exists in the present moment and when we are no longer exclusively identified with a self or with an outcome of any kind.

This book points to the possibility of waking up out of the darkness of the separate self, which expresses itself as confusion, disconnection, fear, and misery. There is a possibility to wake up out of our traumas, fixations and addictions, pain and suffering, grief and loss, our self-importance, and even the pursuit of awakening itself. It is to realize and live the already existing interconnectedness of this moment. Awakening isn't reserved for the special few; it's an opportunity for us all. Awakening is our birthright.

May you reclaim your birthright and awaken to the light that is already ignited within.

In Being, Brian

Always remember, truth cannot be said, it can be shown. It is a finger pointing to the moon. All words are just fingers pointing to the moon, but don't accept the fingers as the moon. The moment you start clinging to the fingers – that's where doctrines, cults, creeds, dogmas, are born – then you have missed the whole point. The fingers were not the point; the point was the moon.

- Osho

Table of Contents

Dedication v

In Loving Gratitude vii

A Note About the Book ix

An Invitation from the Author xi

Introduction: Eclipsed by Fear xix

Part 1 – Nondual Awakening: A Journey into Oblivion 1
    Chapter 1: Under the Influence of the Separate Self. 5

Part 2 – The Moon of Awakening: The Four Keys to Self-
Realization 11
    Chapter 1: Surrender: Letting Go into What Is. 14
    Chapter 2: The Art of Taking No Position .18
    Chapter 3: Original Inactivity: It's All up to Grace 21
    Chapter 4: The "I" is the Cosmic Joke: Embracing
        Divine Humour 24

Part 3 – The New Moon of Awakening: Waking Up Out
of the Dream of Separation and Dealing with Our Pain. 27
    Chapter 1: Transforming the River of Shame 30
    Chapter 2: Freedom From the Rusty Cage of Doubt 36
    Chapter 3: Buried in the Graveyard of Desire 41
    Chapter 4: Fornicating Towards Wholeness: Transforming
        Sex Addiction. 46
    Chapter 5: Waking Up Out of the Black Hole of Trauma 62

Part 4 – The First Quarter Moon: The Challenge of Embodied
Awakening in Everyday Life 73
    Chapter 1: Embracing Aloneness in Relationships: Moving
        Beyond Family Obligations and Social Contracts 75

Chapter 2: Embracing Mother Kali: The Destroyer of
Codependent Relationships.................................82
Chapter 3: Wide Awake Around the Water Cooler: Taking
Down the Petty Tyrant at Work............................93
Chapter 4: Pseudo Digital Enlightenment: The Problem of
Facebook Questing and WiFi Awakeness 102
Chapter 5: Like a Glacial Mountain, Unmoved.................109

**Part 5 – Full Moon Fever: Facing Death, Grief, Hell,
and Nonbeing** 117
Chapter 1: Every Moment is Complete as It is: A Rolodex
of Transformation and Release 119
Chapter 2: The Moon in the Gutter: Transforming the Terror
of a Horrifying Death Experience..........................127
Chapter 3: Revisiting Jacobs Ladder: Addiction, Hell, and You ...135
Chapter 4: Radical Acceptance: Grief as a Gateway to
Nondual Being...145

**Part 6 – The Last Quarter of Awakening: Popular Problems
of a Spiritual Seeking Kind** 153
Chapter 1: Untying the Devotional Knot of Suffering 155
Chapter 2: On Suffering From a Bad Case of "Zen Sickness".....161
Chapter 3: Destined for "Failurehood" and Hopelessness:
Embracing the Wisdom of Defeat..........................166
Chapter 4: Locked in Frustration: Chasing the Illusion of a
24-Hour Ecstasy...174

Epilogue: Just a Wandering Cosmic Nobody 181
References 185

Introduction: Eclipsed by Fear

> *Zeus, the father of the Olympic Gods, turned mid-day into night, hiding the light of the dazzling Sun; and sore fear came upon men.*
>
> - Archilochus, Greek poet

To gaze up in the sky and witness the cosmic beauty of a solar eclipse is a spectacular event. I've seen the eclipse only once in my life, and I was left baffled and speechless. There is something hauntingly beautiful about it. In many spiritual circles, eclipses represent a catalyst for significant spiritual change, transformation, and personal awakening. They are a cosmic event in nature, full of potential and possibility, and are regarded as an expression of the divine. They are powerful, illuminating, and facilitate dramatic changes in one's consciousness that are often quite sudden and unexpected, leaving one permanently transformed as a result. And for me, the eclipse represents a sudden shift in perception I experienced several years ago while travelling through Europe with my wife, Nadine. One moment I was looking through the lens of the self, and the next, I became a vast expansive awareness. The accompanying fear and terror were profound.

At the time, I had been embracing a journey of awakening for well over a decade and came to believe that I had found the peace and freedom I was looking for. I thought I was awakened until one day when it all came tumbling down. A sudden and profound shift in identity occurred in the most ordinary of events. My wife and I were staying in the beautiful town of Lucerne, Switzerland, and while I was comfortably reading a newspaper in the hotel room, the familiar sense of "me," my personal identity called Brian, just disappeared. Poof! Just like that, "I" vanished. The sense of "me" instantly vaporized. I wasn't meditating. I wasn't contemplating the empty nature of existence. I was casually reading the sports page of the newspaper, hoping they printed last night's NHL scores. The suddenness of it was striking. I have had experiences of dissolving into unity consciousness or experiencing the empty nature of existence and myself before, but this was dramatically different. It was a total and complete absence of a *self*, me, my world, and of everything that gave me the familiar felt sense of being "Brian."

My whole sense of self was eclipsed by a vast black abyss. It was so totally black. I felt like I had no way of pinpointing where I began and where I ended; there was no reference point in which to define myself. The moment I realized the absence of my *self*, I instantly felt like I was receding and spiralling backwards into what appeared to be a black hole. Something completely impersonal had taken over. The process was out of my control. But I was aware, not through the usual perceptual lens of being "Brian," but of an impersonal awareness that was beyond the identity of "Brian." I sat on the bed in a state of "frozenness," physically still, and wide-eyed with the realization that there was most definitely a body here, but there was no "me" that felt located inside it. It was so uncanny it was shocking to say the least. Strangely, as I continued to recede further into the black hole, everything I could

Every Evening Comes the Moon

sense and everything I could see and hear, became flat and one dimensional. There was a deafening silence that filled my ears. The silence appeared louder than the traffic noises I could hear outside through the hotel window. I could hear the silence over the hustle and bustle of the city. It was so strange and beyond comprehension. All outside noise became the background as this black abyss energy enveloped me and completely took the foreground of my experience. I imagine that if someone had walked into the room at this point, they would have seen me simply sitting there completely still, immobile, wide-eyed, and appearing to be focused on something. I'm not entirely sure if I could have been capable of responding verbally if I was asked a question, yet I was fully aware and conscious of everything happening, but "I" was just not there. In the stark absence of "me," a sudden wave of fear and terror emerged in my being. What started off as a receding backwards now appeared to be a tumbling type of experience. There was nothing to brace my fall, no soft-landing spot, or nothing I could call safe and secure. I was in a total free-fall.

I have no idea how much time had passed during my ordeal, but as Nadine returned from her walk in the city, she looked at me and knew something was up. She asked me what was going on, and I had no idea how to reply. I did not get into the specifics of what was happening to me as I did not fully understand it myself, so I asked if we could just sit in silence together. I tried to relax that evening, but all I could sense was this continual descent in each and every moment, with no apparent end in sight. As I slept, I felt like I was hovering; although my body was asleep, I felt very much awake and not in need of sleep. I was scared to go to sleep, believing I would not wake up again. As morning came, I began journaling about my experiences and found the process relieving as I started to feel grounded and centered. I wrote and wrote; words poured forth, revealing insights and revelations, particularly shining light on the blind spots in my journey of awakening. For example, although I had experienced many personal shifts and transformations in consciousness, it hit me just how much spiritual knowledge and concepts I used and parroted as my own from other spiritual teachers and teachings, instead of them coming from my own direct experiences. There is talking about emptiness, but to dive to the depths of it and suddenly let go of everything I thought I was, is an entirely different thing. This was not merely conceptual thinking. It felt like an energetic insight had rippled throughout my body as I wrote and re-read the words in my journal. I gleaned that the descent into the abyss I had experienced the other day and that continued to occur as I wrote; the spontaneous nature of it chipped away at parts of myself I had not owned up to or seen through yet. And even though I found some temporary reprieve through my writing, a mixture of insights and frightening experiences would take place for the remainder of my trip.

For several evenings, I experienced disturbing dreams of being tortured and participating in the torture of others, and of intense desires and fantasies which appeared all too real. The fear continued, and my wife was finding my company distant and unpleasant. As we entered Germany, the experiences started to intensify. I felt like I was energetically sensitive to different parts of the country when we travelled it, which is not uncommon for most people visiting Germany, given the violent history, but I was plagued by more and more disturbing dreams where I was being forced to witness the atrocities that were committed there. Again, I was the one being burned alive and the one subjecting others to be placed in the ovens. I was both the victim and the perpetrator. It felt so real. It was terrifying. I was starting to feel desperate. It wasn't until we were in Bruges, Belgium that I wrote in my journal. '*You just have to go with it; stop running, whatever is happening, remember, just go with it.*' These words seemed to come from nowhere, and as simple as they were, I started to feel a sense of relief as I followed my inner guidance. My energy and attention started to relax. I stopped panicking and trying to figure out my situation. I felt guided to stop managing my fear and terror, and in doing so, I experienced something odd; I experienced paradox and the possibility of realizing the light within the dark, the healing within the pain, and the clarity within the confusion. The more attention and focus I gave to the disturbing images, the more real they became. So, when my awareness relaxed, the images started to fade away and lose their pull on me. I felt like I could relax a little more and be more open to my situation. I stopped judging my internal experiences. My whole world was caving in and losing its solidity and definition, meaning, and significance, but I did not feel like I was resisting or fearing it as much anymore. This allowed me to trust the process and integrate deeper dimensions of my being.

Soon after, we returned home to Canada, and I continued to feel a sense of freedom in the midst of the unknown and saw that existence had opened up tremendously to me, revealing a vast terrain of unchartered consciousness and energies I had never experienced before. It would take me many years to fully digest, understand, and integrate this experience in my life, but I gleaned that difficult and frightening experiences in life can be met and felt from a place of freedom and surrender rather than a place of terror and contraction. Even our most terribly frightening experiences hold the essence of freedom and healing. At some point along the awakening journey, we must face the fear of nothingness and pass through it.

Next, in Part I, let's take a closer look at what is meant by nondual awakening through the story of Gautama the Buddha.

Part 1 – Nondual Awakening: A Journey into Oblivion

Give yourself no name, no shape. In the darkness and the silence reality is found.

- Nisargadatta Maharaj

Nondual awakening literally means "not two." Meaning, existence isn't given to us twice, or to put it another way, nothing is separate. Everything – and I mean everything, is interconnected. Everything is an expression of love. Nondual awakening is waking up to this realization, which is the nature of who we are. To realize the interconnectedness of everything is to realize their absolute nothingness. To awaken is to have passed through oblivion, the fundamental nothingness that we are. Awakening is a total demolition job. An inner demolition job. Everything we have come to believe about ourselves and the world around us changes dramatically; in fact, it all comes to an end. That is, the exclusive identification with a separate self comes to an end. The act of identifying with an "I" ceases. It's the end of identification with a separate little self that creates. It is the end of illusion. Awakening is seeing through this lie of separateness, this deception we have sustained through unchecked beliefs and assumptions about who and what we really are. The seeing through of this illusion reveals *that* which is always already here; a vast impersonal awareness that is prior to everything, before the mind, body, and the world, and yet, it is none other than the mind, body, and world at large. Awakening is a paradoxical realization. Call it enlightenment, source, wholeness, nirvana, God or consciousness, *that* which was there before your birth and is ever-present here and now while reading this book, and which will be here after your death, is what I am pointing to. But the "you," who you think you are, who I am, can't see it or even know it because it is beyond the thinking mind. It is like the physical eye trying to see itself. It's impossible. It is beyond all comprehension. One can only ever be *it*, one can only be *that* which *it* already *is*. Seeing through the self and the illusion we have bought into for so many years is a surrender into this present moment, just as it is. It is a *let-go* into what is. *That* which is alive and awake right now requires no effort to know itself because it simply is. Awakening is waking up into the suchness and simplicity of what is.

Many people, just like you, are waking up to who they are in their ordinary everyday life. There are many accounts of people waking up in the most mundane and unexpected events, like sitting casually on a park bench, walking through a field, driving a car, or even stepping onto a bus. There are also the accounts of individuals waking up while struggling in the gutters of existence such as addictions, trauma, and abuse. Awakening can happen to anyone at any time and any place, and the entrance fee is yourself. We just need to take the plunge into the black abyss of *no-self*.

A Journey into Oblivion

Siddhartha Gautama (the Buddha) took such a plunge and passed through the fear and terror of *no-self*, and having faced his own demons and desires, woke up to his true nature. Despite being a wealthy and having had every personal need met while also being sheltered from all forms of suffering, a powerful urge to seek his true nature emerged when he witnessed four events. An old man walking, a sick man struggling, a corpse being carried off to the pyre, and finally, a man dressed in ochre robes – a spiritual seeker.

It was the sight of the spiritual seeker that ignited his inner quest and pursuit for truth. Having witnessed the fragility of old age, the suffering of the sick, and the inevitability of death, he realized he too was going to encounter the same fate, that he too, by nature of simply being human, would grow old, get sick, and die. It was the sight of the spiritual seeker that grabbed his attention though. The seeker within realized something of the *deathless*, something inside him that could never die, and it was this experience which manifested an intense desire and urgency within Siddhartha to pursue and realize the truth of his being. He left the peace and security of his family and the comforts of living in the kingdom and stacked his whole life for the mystery of existence to reveal itself. He embarked on the quest for enlightenment. He descended into the depths of his soul and dived into the unknown with no life preservers. He experimented with every meditation under the sun and sought out the most respected spiritual gurus throughout the land. He spent many years meditating, practicing, reading, and contemplating, but enlightenment continued to allude him.

After many years of seeking and failing at achieving awakening, he decided to stop. He decided to stop seeking and made the decision to sit down under a Bodhi tree, refusing to move or get up until he realized Truth. He surrendered fully. He gave up all effort at trying to be awakened. Here, he started to see that it was desire which prevented him from awakening; it was personal effort that kept that *which is* at bay. By doing nothing, he saw through the desire for material and bodily existence and the desire for spiritual enlightenment. His commitment was total. He willingly laid his head on the cosmic gelatin and died to all of his personal attachments, fears, and desires. He let go and fell freely into the abyss. Fear and desire were burned up in the fire of awareness. Falling further, he was enticed by the Gods with temptations in various forms and repelled ferocious demons. Nothing would move him. His awareness did not flicker, and he did not get pulled into any form of personal identification, and then suddenly, everything became radiantly clear and obvious to him. Awakening is always sudden. He saw that there is no such thing as a separate definable self. And if there is *no-self,* who could possibly Awaken then? No effort was needed to see this; it was so abundantly obvious. Realization hides in plain sight. We are always already awake.[i]

Buddha's awakening story is an invitation for us all. And like the Buddha, we need to sacrifice it all; we must forego the image of ourselves and the world we hold in mind. We are invited to pass through the fear and terror of *no-self.* Awakening to our true nature is both beautiful and ruthless because it asks us to give up and let go of everything we have used to define ourselves. The journey is not always revealed in a nice and neat little package. Actually, it rarely ever is. Awakening is not about becoming a better person or improving our lot in life. The journey is about the death of the self. But in death there is resurrection. By losing everything, we gain everything, not as a separate self but as Truth. By dying to the self, we see the interconnecting thread of existence in everything and everyone. Everyone is seen to be a manifestation of ourselves, and we *know* we are not separate from anything and everything. Everyone manifests from *truth* as we are none other than Truth. To live from this realization is what it means to be truly human. To live from *truth* is to live as love itself since the truth of ourselves is in everything and everyone we encounter. Nothing is excluded.

Chapter 1: Under the Influence of the Separate Self

> *'Suppose I told you I was an addict...' I said. 'Well, everybody in the room is an addict, actually.' Not necessarily an addict to drugs or gambling or alcohol but mainly to 'me' – we are all addicted to the drug of 'me' and all that comes with it.*
>
> - Tony Parsons

We are all drunk on the self. We are under the influence of our fears and desires and driven to define ourselves, to give us some sense of personal definition. We are drunk on being separate, unconscious and unaware, lost and deluded. This is all we have ever known because it is all we have ever been taught. We only need to look at the evening news to get a felt sense of this. The never-ending global wars, incessant greed and corruption and atrocities inflicted on one another in the pursuit of "protecting our freedoms" run rampant. We live in a hyper-individualized society, which is strongly supported and encouraged, where one's moment-to-moment experience is self-motivated. Believing exclusively in the self leaves one's being frozen and contracted, where we are imprisoned by our thoughts and ideas about who and what we are. This is my life. This is my career. This is my family. I'm Canadian. I'm a therapist. I'm a politician. I'm depressed. Or better yet, I'm a nondual teacher, and I have spiritual experiences. Mine, mine, mine! And around and around we go, constantly defining, re-defining, and defending ourselves in each and every moment.

Every action seems to serve the self to fuel its desires and wants and reject that which is perceived to be threatening to its survival. "Me" and "mine" seem to be the Global Mantra, particularly in North America. It is like a constant vibrational hum endlessly repeated amongst ourselves and preached to our children. The cult of "me" is a shared global religion, and it is the root cause of our suffering. We are so deeply alienated from the truth of who and what we are as human beings. We so freely identify with our thoughts, feelings, and images that we never think to question them. We take them to be reality. And the idea of surrendering and exposing the dualistic relationship of "me and my world" is so terrifying to the self. Who would I be without my sense of identity, name, culture, or sense of family and place in this world? How would I even live my life?

This is the life of a contracted self, and it is dictated by time and illustrated with a beginning, middle, and end. For me, the narrative went something like this: I was born in 1977 and I will experience as much as I can in life before I die. I will wear my experiences like badges on my sleeve (successful career, wife, status, trustworthy, dependable) while showcasing them to my friends and family just to prove how important and successful I have become. There was a time where I bought into this script and lived life from this place at a feverish pace. I did not know it at the time, but I experienced life as a bundled-up little knot, tied up in my own thoughts and perceptions about how life should be and the various ways in which I defined myself. I thought I was unique and special and carried this persona in various ways and into my relationships with family and friends. In my early to late teenage years, I used my artistic skills as a way of being seen and validated, winning art awards and attending art camps, and when that dried up, I morphed into being a scuba diving beach bum. When that lost its juice, I pursued academics and studied addictions counselling. Although this had a more authentic feel to it, I was still perpetuating the self and desired mirroring and recognition. I used my mother's struggles with mental health as a means of defining my uniqueness and specialness in the helping profession. And when this was quickly exposed, I dived into the ultimate identity quest: that of being a spiritual seeker. I received a lot of mirroring mileage from this one – I milked it for all it was worth. I engaged in over-energized discussions about *being-ness* and spiritual transcendence coupled with a bevy of attending spiritual workshops and trainings, which dominated my life. I was in hot pursuit of spiritual transcendence, and I thought this was the real freedom to be had. I was hooked.

We are so in love with who we believe ourselves to be, the image of ourselves we want to present to the world, and how we would like to be seen by others. But as we begin to sober up and glimpse our awakened truth, the questions become, "How far am I willing to go? Do I fall back into a self-imposed stupor or do I begin to wake up to who I am?"

In the movie, *The Matrix*, Neo (played by Keanu Reeves) was faced with such a similar question when he encountered Morpheus – an awakened being:

"Morpheus: The Matrix is everywhere. It is all around us. Even now, in this very room. You can see it when you look out your window or when you turn on your television. You can feel it when you go to work, or when you go to church, or when you pay your taxes. It is the world that has been pulled over your eyes to blind you from the truth.

Neo: What truth?

Morpheus: That you are a slave, Neo. Like everyone else, you were born into bondage, born inside a prison that you cannot smell, taste, or touch. A prison for your mind. Unfortunately, no one can be told what the Matrix is. You have to see it for yourself. This is your last chance. After this, there is no turning back. You take the blue pill and the story ends. You wake up in your bed and believe whatever you want to believe. You take the red pill and you stay in Wonderland and I show you how deep the rabbit-hole goes. Remember – all I am offering is the truth, nothing more."[ii]

If we truly slow ourselves down and contemplate our situation, we may notice an intuitive knowing that we are not meant to live in a constant state of separation. If we follow our intuition and see just how far the rabbit hole goes, we may very well wake up. If we feel the pull to awaken, we must go all the way. To abort self-realization is to endure a great deal of suffering. To experience the truth and yet consciously chose to live in an illusion is a traumatic split in consciousness. If we have a taste of the Truth, there is no turning back. As the great sage Ramana Maharshi once said, 'Your head is already in the Tiger's mouth. There is no escape.'[iii] The journey of awakening illuminates everything in existence, from our lack of clarity and unconscious obsessions to the darker pockets of human existence and even non-ordinary states of existence. It is an endless fall into a black hole where all of our conscious and unconscious attachments become intensely magnified. The gritty and shadowy aspects of our consciousness not only scream to the surface of awareness but demand our attention and recognition. And so too does the cosmic realm open one up to the energies at a cosmic level, where demons and idols we have loved and feared all come out to play by manifesting through dreams and visitations. Rather than grasp at survival-hood and beg for hope and security, the invitation has always been to let go and plunge all the way into the abyss of *no-self*, with no expectations and to be with whatever arises.

In some ways, Neo is today's updated version of the Buddha. "The Chosen One," as he is often referred to in the Matrix movies, and like Buddha, he left the comforts of his life and sought Truth. The moment he swallowed the red pill, existence opened itself up – illuminating both the beauty and the terror. The more we descend into the rabbit hole, the more we experience the truth of existence. We see how we have been living a complete lie. Shockingly, it is as if we have dined on the bland buffet of separateness for so long and for so many lives, that we have lost our palate for eternity and now only realized it. We have lost the flavor of sharing the gift of infiniteness in everyday life. The deeper we live this truth, the more it becomes abundantly clear we can no longer return to the world of lies and deceit, buying into the world of separation and otherness any longer. It is a profound shift. No more can we stomach the lies of identification and separateness, and in seeing through illusion and fixation from moment to moment, dying to the death of "me" and "my life," and resting in the fathomless black unknown, we come back to our true home in the cosmos.

Now, it's time to grab a glass of water, take the red pill, and continue down the rabbit hole.

Part 2 – The Moon of Awakening: The Four Keys to Self-Realization

> *He who is able to make the full moon rise in the sky of the darkest night, has a right to claim the glory of the three worlds – the heaven, the earth and the nether spheres.*
>
> - Baul Mystics

I have been mesmerized by the beauty and power of the moon since I can remember. I have spent many days and nights camping solo in the backcountry of Manitoba all year long. During those hot summer days and long, bone-chilling winter nights, the one constant companion I had was the brilliancy of the moon. Even on those cloudy days, I knew it was there; I just had to wait for a little bit to finally witness its illuminating brilliance peeking through the clouds. I felt surrounded by a beautiful mystery where everything was magnified with such intensity, and the silence and stillness were deafening. Shadows would dance among the shoreline rocks and within the dense forests. Movements could be heard just in the brush, and wolf calls echoed across the lake. Removed from civilization, I was alone and at the mercy of mother nature and my own thoughts. I was left to myself. And as the evenings become longer, the night becomes darker, and when darkness descends, our own inner darkness can present itself. Our pain and unconscious arise, and we only have the light of the moon and our awareness to guide us. I had that in the evenings. When we encounter our inner darkness, there exists the possibility of transformation. In our aloneness, we are confronted with ourselves, our pains, fears, and life of division and separateness. In the heart of darkness exists the possibility of waking up.

I liken the moon to that of our true nature. The moon is ever-present, day and night, and although there are times when we cannot see it with the naked eye, it is always there. And like the moon, the one constant companion along the journey of self-realization is that of awareness, our true being, no matter what is present before us. Awareness is always here and now. That which we encounter in life is simply an invitation to realize its presence. In this second part, I use the four main cycles of the moon: new moon (also known as the dark moon), first quarter moon (also known as half-moon), full moon, and the last quarter moon phases as metaphors in pointing to the awakening process. Each phase of the moon represents a collection of experiences that can be had along the journey towards wholeness.

Like the cycles of the moon, awakening is an endless, moment-to-moment unfolding. There is no final arrival point with awakening. How awake you are at this moment is what matters. Because here's the thing, even though you may have had a direct recognition of your divine condition, you can get pulled back into the dream state of separation and self-identification at any time. The well-known nondual teacher, Papaji, was famous for saying, "Awakening is moment-to-moment, right up until your last breath." But before we explore the various experiences found along the way towards self-realization, let's first take a look at four key qualities that allow for the recognition of our true condition – that of surrender, the art of taking no position, leaving it all up to grace, and embracing divine humor. Awakening is not a "how-to" approach; rather, it is more of a *let-go* into experience. These four essential keys illuminate the moon of awakening, allowing any experience we are having to be a workable situation and potential opportunity for awakening. Embracing these four keys is a hallmark of an awakened life. They show us that our lives do not have to be a struggle.

Chapter 1: Surrender: Letting Go into What Is

To yield is to be preserved whole.

- Lao Tzu

The first transformational key in self-realization is that of surrender. To identify as the self is to clench at life. It is to move through life like a tight fist, resisting, fighting, and constantly managing our experiences. Bound we are and bound we will die. Contraction is not our natural state of being; it is a fear-based state of separateness, lacking love and fullness. We have been taught that surrender means defeat, that we have given up. We typically think of surrender as an experience of having no energy, no control, and no real freedom. It is assumed freedom is found through the belief in a separate self, always vying for safety and security. This couldn't be further from the truth. We need to do a complete 180-degree turn and experience a fundamental shift in our being. When we let go, we have arrived; when we are defeated, we have found. It is a paradoxical truth that happens through surrender.

Have you ever noticed life has a natural way of unfolding when you relax and let go into your experience? Have you ever struggled to remember something, like where you put your car keys and have looked everywhere, searching desperately in all the places you typically leave them? And, the moment when you stopped looking and when you relaxed and stopped trying to remember, that is the moment you suddenly remembered where you put them? It's a small example, but surrender is like that. When we get out of our own way, existence shows up. When we stop trying to achieve, we have arrived; we have awakened. To get a deeper felt sense of this experience, allow yourself at this moment to relax your attention on your inner experiences, that of your thoughts, emotions, sensations, ideas, images, and your body. Relax the hold you have on them, meaning, allow attention to these inner states and experiences to soften and dissolve completely. Notice that your inner experiences may still be there, but the energy of attention is gone. Notice the simplicity of being without holding on to the body and mind. Notice the spaciousness and ability to let go. Here, we can drop the body and mind through the power of surrender and feel the depth of our being, untouched and completely free. The invitation is to live from this place in our everyday life, to surrender and let go in each moment and be so totally free.

We are involved in a never-ending process of change and transformation. It is the eternal law of existence. What arises must dissolve. The wave is never separate from the ocean. It is all one. While surfing the waves of existence, we must surrender to the flow and natural current of life. Nothing is fixed in life; there is no solid footing upon which we can stand and claim that will give us absolute safety, security, and certainty in this life. The more we relax, the more we see that the activity of attention and fixation creates a sense of constriction and separation. There is no "you" doing the surrendering – this is important to see. There is no "I" who is surrendering to an experience because that would just be another illusion. We would be stuck in the same trap of self-identification. Surrendering is more of a spontaneous happening arising from a deep trust in existence. From a place of deep acceptance, we surrender the bound-up energy found in the patterns of narrow fixations on thoughts, feelings, images, sensations, and the body itself. We relax the hold we have on our internal states and external obsessions. It can be quite astonishing to see just how much of our life energy we use to maintain a state of separation and defensiveness. When we live as "mind," we drain our potential and abandon the truth of who we are. The notion of the self, the idea, and image we have as "me," is surrendered, and life continues as it is.

When we surrender and let go into our feelings, we do not deny them; we do not attempt to make them go away or even heal or change them. We simply surrender to them in such a way that they are allowed to be there in the moment. If fear arises, we surrender to it and feel it fully. If thoughts arise, we don't try to make them go away; we simply see them as they are without the habit energy of fixation. Even with our bodies, we can suspend our attention, grasp, and relax beyond it. If there is physical pain or pleasure, it's no problem; we are boundless and no longer interpret our experiences. By surrendering, we are much more spontaneous and creative in our responses. To be surrendered is to be involved in eternity, completely letting go of each and every moment and involved in life but totally unaffected by it at the deepest level of our being. We are in deep cooperation with existence when we are surrendered; we experience flow, gratitude, ease, and connectivity. Existence passes through us freely and uninterrupted. It is an experience being lived and guided by a force beyond our mind's perceptions and senses. It is like we are a hollow flute, empty of the self while playing our own song. When we attempt to fixate ourselves and define our consciousness in some way, we become hard and heavy and incapable of flow and free being. When we attempt to escape the *what is* of the moment, we suffer. Surrender is freedom, and from this realization, our situation transforms. What was once perceived to be a problem is now seen to be only another manifestation in consciousness. We stop accumulating things or even creating problems out of our personal experiences. When surrendered, we cooperate with life.

The key of surrender allows us to open up to life and meet it – all of it, in a clear and undefended way. When surrendered, we can't be defeated – how can someone who has already surrendered be defeated? Here, we are better able to bob and weave through life's endless manifestations. The paradox is that in surrendering we are much more available to life, the people around us, and the world at large. We are more in tune with our being, relaxed, and grounded. We are openly available to each moment and can respond from a place of openness and heartfelt compassion. Surrender brings forth an abundance of love and compassion in the situations we happen to find ourselves in. We are curious and gentle with ourselves. As we relax more into the moment of *what is*, the fist of separateness unclenches, and we abide deeper into being.

Chapter 2: The Art of Taking No Position

When the heart is at peace, for and against are forgotten.

- Chang Tzu

The second key is no judgment. It is the art of taking no position towards life and all experiences, both high and low. Nothing is denied, nor is anything grasped. Everything is allowed to be as it is. The art of taking no position is the art of accepting the mystery of life as it is. No judgement means no judgement, which includes not judging your judgements. The slightest flicker of condemnation towards our experiences throws us back into separation and suffering. It's important to see this isn't a passive nondual gaze where one is hiding out in the void, disconnected from life, but of one who is fully participating in life. If fear arises, it's accepted. If anger arises, it's allowed. If desire emerges, it's not made into a problem. There is no moral code here. Taking no position goes beyond conventional morals and ethics because the space of "no judgement" goes beyond the mind itself. Morals are created because people are not living their true condition. Morals exist because people are living as though they are separate. In "no judgement," there is a clear space of awareness where things are seen as they are. When things are seen for what they are, that life is simply energy in motion, everything arises and falls on its own. When we stop hiding from fear or chasing desires and allow the energy of such emotions to be there as they are, in the moment, they dissolve on their own. We don't actually have to do anything with them but simply allow them free space to run their course. These are the peaks and valleys of living. The peaks are the high-end joyful experiences in life; the intense, loving, and exuberant times, and the valleys are that of confusion and pain, misery and suffering. Taking no position towards either of them is seeing the impermanence of experience and the illusion of the self. If we happen to find ourselves in a state of deep pain or even madness, we allow it, and we stay with it with an open heart. Whatever the thought, whatever the emotion or state of consciousness, all is accepted and allowed. The Zen master Sosan once said:

The Great Way is not difficult for those who have no preferences. When love and hate are both absent everything becomes clear and undisguised. Make the smallest distinction, however, and heaven and earth are set infinitely apart. If you wish to see the truth then hold no opinion for or against. The struggle of what one likes and what one dislikes is the disease of the mind. [iv]

Have you noticed life becomes much more fluid and easy when we stop making a problem out of our experiences, especially emotionally turbulent experiences? When we get out of our own way, drop our inner commentary and criticalness, and simply allow things to be, the mysteries of existence can naturally reveal themselves. It is where spontaneous insights and healing take place. The world of "should" and "should not's" disappears and is replaced by a relaxed naked awareness which witnesses the arising and falling of the unmanifest and manifest world. Life is lived with ease.

Awakening is really about being okay with the present moment. It's that simple. The moment I take a position for or against is the moment I have resurrected the self. The moment my awareness contracts around an experience is the moment I have given it life. My experiences filter through my preferences, and my preferences are another way of manipulating the moment. It is a self-preservation technique that ultimately fails. Problems only exist when we are bound up in an exclusive identification with a self – no self, no problem. When we let go of how things should be, the possibility of seeing and being with that which is not touched by the ecstasies and horrors of life arises. The depth of taking no preference knows no end. It's fathomless. Even when faced with extremely difficult situations like the loss of a job, going through a divorce, or facing a life-threatening illness, we don't see it as a problem. We are not making a problem out of our problems. We may go to marriage counselling or take the proper course of medical treatments recommended by our doctors, but we are no longer making a problem out of our situation.

Because just like the key of surrender, the art of taking no position is not a spiritual philosophy or a meditative technique. It is not about cultivating character or non-ordinary states of consciousness. The art of taking no position is about seeing through the one that could take a position in the first place. No position points to the extinction of the self. No position is Nirvana itself. When the mind is uninvolved in choice, life simply shows up in its entirety and is met with an open and clear heart.

Chapter 3: Original Inactivity: It's All up to Grace

> *Grace is all around us, if we only have the eyes to see it. The good moments are grace, the difficult moments are grace, the confusing moments are grace.*
>
> - Adyashanti

Grace is the third key to awakening. For me, grace would arrive when I was completely defeated and bottomed out, had no more to give, and when I felt completely at a loss, confused, and frightened. When I had no one or nothing else to turn to, grace would suddenly reveal itself. I didn't realize it at the time, but grace arrived in the form of a heavy depression. In my first year of an addictions counselling degree, while participating in a counselling lab session where developing counsellors were expected to do their personal journey work in a group setting, I experienced deep-seated pain. With a heavy blanket draped over me, I curled up in the middle of the circle in the group room. My chest tightened up like a vice grip with tremendous fear and terror racing throughout my body. The fear was intense. There was an inner image of seeing myself descending to the bottom of the ocean, waving and thrashing about. I thought I was going to die. I felt like I was going to go mad. I experienced the pain of many years of isolation, suffering, and feeling like an outcast. The years of suppressing the pain of growing up, affected by the ravages of family mental health and substance use, erupted. It was such an intense experience requiring several years of intensive therapy. Briefly, I even considered dropping out of the program. At that moment, if you were to say this was a moment of grace, I probably would have punched you. But looking back at it now, of all the pain involved and all the struggle I experienced, I see it as one of the most pivotal moments in my life, because it forced me to look within myself and begin the journey of self-discovery and realization. Without that experience, I would have continued to live in pain and blamed others for my state in life. It's amazing, looking back at that experience, it feels like a lifetime ago.

Grace typically announces itself when we least expect it. I didn't see grace amid my pain as I always attributed it to positive experiences and revelations. It took some time before I could fully appreciate the opportunity and transformational power of a difficult and terrifying experience. Through death, loss, fear, and grief, grace revealed itself. Interestingly enough, when I stopped fighting with my experiences, grace would show up. Grace exposes the unreality of living as a separate bound self. Grace is found within our most disturbing experiences, but only if we are open and able to receive it. Grace descends when we are open to life, surrendered, and not grasping. When we are in a state of complete *let-go*, grace reveals itself. Grace is in seeing that we are not in control of anything.

What grabs my interest is how grace arrives in the gutters of existence. Have you noticed this in your own life? Have you noticed a difficult time in your life that became a pivotal transformational opportunity? The beauty of grace is that it is entirely impersonal and beyond the ideas of hope and success. It has nothing to do with the mind, and it's beyond anything we can ever expect. Grace reveals what it is we need to realize at the moment. You see, grace opens us up to existence. Everything we have ever relied on falls apart in the light of grace. Here, we are completely vulnerable and open, and we can either recoil in the face of grace or see it as a gift of transcendence. Grace is available *now*. When we drop our fears, desires, and stories about who we are, grace arrives. When we cease maintaining our suffering, projecting ourselves into the future, and resurrecting the past, grace arrives. All we need to do is get out of our own way and let divinity take over.

Grace arrives through insights, images, visions, and non-ordinary experiences. Essentially, grace arrives as a breaking through of the mind. It is beyond effort of any kind. Grace descends when the mind cannot handle it anymore, when it loses its grasp on reality and its sense of security and self-hood. When the mind is on the brink of despair and confusion and is completely lost, grace arrives. It is a space of total unknowingness, and within that spaciousness lies the potential and fertile ground for transformational opportunity. We have no idea how or what will happen through the process of grace.

Grace is a form of inactivity, an absence of personal will. Life is simply happening and everything is a spontaneous expression. When there is no mind, things get done and life accomplishes itself. This happens in professional sports when athletes lose themselves in it. Each player becomes one. If you really inquire into an experience, it's only after it has taken place that the belief of "I experienced that" or "I did that" comes in. Ownership of an experience happens after the fact. There is no self apart from experience. They are all one and the same. So who could possibly claim ownership of an experience? There simply appears to be a self that is doing; there simply appears to be a self that is experiencing. We have all experienced this at one time or another. However, when we rest in *non-doing*, the mind is suspended, and something greater than the self appears. Life presents itself, and life is what responds to life when uncluttered by the mind.

Chapter 4: The "I" is the Cosmic Joke: Embracing Divine Humour

---

*Enlightenment is to be restored to Divine humour,
to realize that nothing is necessary. No experience is necessary.
You can either become distracted by experience and
repeat it, or you can transcend it.*

- Adi Da

The image of the laughing Buddha points to the last and fourth key of self-realization. Walk into any spirituality bookstore, and you are bound to find a statue of a laughing Buddha sitting in a lotus position with his hands clasped around his big belly, having a big laugh. Life is nothing more than a play of existence. Upon awakening, all the Buddha could do was to have a big belly laugh. He laughed at how obvious it all was. There is no such thing as a self, and he was always already awakened. All personal problems are burnt up in the fire of awakening. Our fears that once were seen as monstrous and overwhelming are now seen as children's tales. We just can't believe in the energetic charge given to some of the most ordinary and inevitable events in life. Divine humour penetrates the seriousness of the mind and allows for the possibility to see through our condition and accept the moment as it is. The mind can't handle paradox, but humour can. Paradox, the merging of life's contradictions, like life and death, good and bad, and right and wrong, overwhelm the mind and bring it to submission. Paradox exposes the unreality of the separate self. The deep belly laugh is in seeing and realizing the chaos of life was never happening to anyone in the first place. Life was nothing personal. This is the hilarity of our situation, and it is where freedom can be found.

The Buddha saw the ridiculousness of his situation and the human condition altogether. He saw how clever the mind was and how we have fallen for an illusion. Once the illusion of "I" is snapped, the belly laugh is spontaneous, deep, and powerful, which echoes throughout one's life. The sense of "I" we were trying to establish or protect never really existed in the first place, and that which we are seeking is already the case. It's such a joke. The belief in a sense of "I," an exclusive identification with "me," is the biggest joke ever played on human existence – a cosmic joke. It's the original joke, and we have all fallen for it. It's brilliant really.

The situation is like this; we have forgotten how to laugh at ourselves and the circumstances we find ourselves in. We have become too self-important, too self-assured, and far too reserved. We restrain ourselves for fear of being too much for other people. We have become too serious. Our whole life is one entire, serious affair. Everything is met with such seriousness and hardship that we lack flow, humour, and playfulness. As the "I," we are always on edge and react to the slightest remark or perceived personal insult. We fail to see the humour of our situation. The Divine humour of being born and identifying as an exclusive independent being, accumulating and consuming as much as we can, defending our property and sense of ownership, only to have it all wiped away by time and the inevitability of death.

The ordinary reactive personality, who is basically in despair and hysterical, can also say that life is meaningless, but such a person is very serious. The Enlightened man, however, Realizes total Freedom. He is no longer serious, but neither is he self-destructive. He has passed into Ecstasy. He has not suppressed or separated from himself-rather, all that he is has been transcended in the Radiant Transcendental Consciousness. Thus, he is full of humor and delight. He is not aggressively opposed to the world, nor is he clinging to it. All the tension in his heart has been re-leased. To speak of Enlightenment without that sign is nonsense.[v]

Divine humour is not a forced humour, nor is it a form of sarcasm. It isn't a callous type of response to life; rather, it is filled with compassion and insight. Divine humour is the ability to be in and navigate the ever-changing paradoxes of life. One day rich, the next day poor, and it is all seen as a non-serious affair. Divine humour brings us back to our ordinariness, seeing that we are nothing special or unique.

The four keys of surrender, taking no position, grace, and divine humour are all hallmarks of an awakened life and allow for awakening to take place in the middle of some of the darkest moments of our human experience. Embracing them penetrates the illusionary nature of the self and facilitates a deeper exploration into the mystery of human existence.

In the next section, I begin with the first phase of the moon cycle – that of the new moon, which represents a collection of themes describing the waking up out of the illusion of the self and dealing with unresolved personal pain and suffering.

Part 3 – The New Moon of Awakening: Waking Up Out of the Dream of Separation and Dealing with Our Pain

---

There is no way around confronting yourself, your unconscious, your fears, your doubts. I myself haven't found any magical way around this. We each have to confront ourselves.

- A. H. Almaas

In returning to my love for camping in the backcountry, in the evening, the moon would either be totally illuminated or cresting, while on other nights, I couldn't see it at all due to the absence of light when the moon sits between the earth and the sun. The blackness of the night would play tricks on my mind; shadows would dance across the shield rock face and along the tree line where I made my camp. I knew the moon was there, but I just didn't have the eyes to see it.

The new moon represents the beginning of a new lunar cycle where the Earth, Moon, and Sun are all positioned in a line. The new moon sits between the earth and the sun, with the sun casting its light on the side of the moon we cannot see. This is why it is also known as the dark moon.[vi] For me, the new moon points to waking up out of our dream of separateness and confronting our unresolved pain. There is a common belief lurking within spiritual communities that once awakening takes place, all the unresolved pain and suffering and one's conditioning is automatically resolved; that all the pain is healed and the sense of separateness is dissolved. This is just another strategy of the mind. You see, awakening is often the easy part; dealing with all of our unresolved pain is the hard part. Getting pulled back into the dream state happens when we avoid dealing with our apparent personal situation. Just because we have realized the truth of our being doesn't mean we will never experience pain or fall back in states of division, confusion, and separateness. We can still be blinded by our pain, fears and desires, and our traumas. We need to bring our newfound gift of awakening to those parts of ourselves that remain in division. This requires us to heal the old wounds from the past and to discriminate between what is *truth* from what is *illusion*. We have to be awake to all aspects of our human condition; to our thoughts, feelings, sensations, our body, and states of consciousness.

There is a tendency to want to run away from our pain, but from the light of awakening, the invitation is to finally face our misery. The new moon represents a turning point in our consciousness where we have had a glimpse of our true being and we long to stay true to ourselves. Here, although we have experienced a sudden awakening, our conditioned beliefs and unresolved pain still remain. The new moon represents the first taste of nondual realization; the beginning of the nondual journey of awakening and transformation. It is the first real glimpse of our true nature. Although, it can be difficult to fully abide in this realization since there remains a great deal of pain lodged within our being. To wake up means we cannot bypass any of our unresolved pain and confusions, and instead, we need to have a genuine encounter with our personal suffering and seek to understand and heal those wounds. After all, it is pain and suffering which can serve to wake us up into deeper aspects of our being.

We begin this part of the book by addressing our internal, painful states, starting with the issue of shame and the self-betrayal of having lived a lie. Here, we will explore the healing of shame within the transformational light of awakened awareness. We will then explore awakening beyond our desires and fixations and discover healing from our addictive acting-out behaviors. Specifically, we will turn our attention to waking up out of sex addiction. Further, we will also address how the experience of doubt is used by the mind to minimize or disregard important insights and transformational experiences as a means of sabotaging or aborting the awakening process. The last chapter will conclude with a peek at the possibility of waking up out of our trauma.

Let's start with transforming the river of shame.

Chapter 1: Transforming the River of Shame

Shame is a soul eating emotion.

\- Carl Jung

At the root of the many people I have worked with therapeutically, lies a deep sense of shame. The wound is so huge it is almost intolerable to deal with. And once awakened to their true nature, many report a felt sense of being inadequate and lacking something real and substantial. They are often shocked at how critical and judgemental they have been toward themselves. Awakening illuminates everything, so much so that our internal states become much more clear and real. Meaning, we see and feel it much more intensely. We lose the strategy of the illusionary mind to buffer against it. Having seen through the illusion of the mind also means seeing through its defenses – at least some of them. John Bradshaw describes that shame by saying:

> *It is not about what I've done, rather, it is about who I am and when I believe that I am nothing more than a loser and a failure, shame becomes toxic. They are so mired in their own shame they are unable to trust themselves and navigate the world. They are a slave to their own internal criticalness.*[vii]

Alongside our internal criticalness, there is another aspect of shame that is important for us to see here. Shame is also about having sold out. It's about having betrayed the essence of who we are. Awakening puts pressure on the illusion of the self, exposing its fundamental unreality, which can be very painful to experience. The veil of the self begins to lift, and we see how we have been living a lie all along, deluded into believing our personal sense of separation and permanence, and while under the spell of illusion, it's not such an easy experience to tolerate. Realizing the empty nature of ourselves and the world we live in, the impermanence of everything, the endless cycles of change and transformation, and the ending of who we originally thought we were, can be devastating. This is where shame expresses itself in a different light. To realize we have been living a lie all these years, that we were living the life of a mirage, a false sense of self, and having lived a completely fake existence; to be a collection of mirrors mirroring back what everyone expected or thought of us, is to live a life as a pretense and can be excruciating. Imagine the hugeness of seeing your entire life as nothing more than that of a fraud, devoid of any real connection, authenticity, *beingness*, and unconditional love.

Exposing the lie of selfhood can feel like we have just been hit by a cosmic freight train. For all of our life, we thought we had been living a true and meaningful existence, only to see it all flash before our eyes. We are shocked at how we have been duped into believing, supporting, and defending something unreal. Shame can serve two purposes here; it is a reaction to the awfulness of having sold ourselves out, and it also acts as a buffer against one's awakening process. A person can hang out in shame – identify with it for a long period of time, never transcend it or fully resolve it, and never experience the deeper dimensions of their awakened being. Shame can give a person a sense of identity, albeit a negative one, but an identity even so. Shame is of the mind, and the mind can use shame as a defense against descending further into the emptiness. A. H. Almaas, the founder of the "Diamond Approach" to self-realization observed this phenomenon while working with students:

> *We always find the student struggling with painful reactions to the emptiness as it is exposed. She feels deficient and inadequate, worthless and unimportant, weak and inferior, a failure, a loser, a nothing. She feels fake and unreal, lacking substance or value. She feels that she is a liar and a deceiver, an imposter. She feels her life has been a hoax, a waste. These feelings and reactions bring up the most painful effect of them all, shame. The student feels ashamed of herself, embarrassed about herself; she wants to hide. The shame is a specific painful feeling of deficiency, exposure and judgment, all related to a sense of inadequacy in being oneself.*[viii]

These are all reactions against emptiness, and they run deep. The harshness of inner judgement, self-criticalness, and self-loathing becomes a very real experience. It can be quite intolerable for some people to deal with as there is a sense of being stuck in a thick boggy marsh with no ability to move, with a loss of insight and realization, connection to their soul, and a loss of connection with others. It can feel like there is no way out. Shame is sustained through our inner critical analysis and self-judgement, thickening the experience of it as it expands and becomes the reality of one's entire being. It can feel like one's whole being is a flow of inner shame, a river of disgrace so thick it's like black tar running throughout one's entire essence. It's sticky and incredibly difficult to get out of. This stickiness is the energy of inner judgement; the more we judge it, the thicker and bigger it becomes. The more real it feels.

The situation becomes desperate. Some people will look towards positive psychology as a means of dealing with their experiences. They will reframe their negative outlook into a more positive self-fulfilling one. It's a futile attempt, though, because both the inner judgment and positive self-talk are all aspects of the same thing, the same illusion - the mind. Even when we trade up for a seemingly more positive and tolerable psychological script, it's still of the mind; it's still an illusion and the issue of shame is not fully resolved.

The way through this dilemma requires a great deal of patience, clarity, and observation. We need to observe how we are creating and sustaining our experience of self-judgement and over-compensation. By noticing the movement of thought, we can see how the energy of it and how we speak to ourselves fuels our experience. Noticing this gives us distance from our inner involvements, allowing us to dis-identify from the mind and rest in Emptiness instead. As we dislodge even more from the mind, the more we can be one with the intense feeling of shame without the associated inner self-talk. Transforming shame is in being with it and allowing it to be as it is with no involvement of the mind. Shame is really just compacted energy, and if we can be with it without any judgement and allow it to be there, shame will dissipate, revealing the underlying nature of emptiness.

Andy's Journey

Andy was someone I had the opportunity to work with for a few sessions. He reported a tremendous amount of shame, feeling fake, and like a fraud. He had recently completed a month-long meditation retreat which exposed the mirage of his life. He felt like a complete fraud at work, within his marriage and his social network. His marriage was built on the idea of success, security, and chasing the image of the "Canadian Dream." The idea of marriage equated to having succeeded in life, despite never having fully loved his partner. In our sessions together, he would go on about how he didn't feel like he knew how to be himself, be real with others, or how to be truly human. He was in a crisis of *being*. I wondered if Andy would see his experience as a transformational opportunity or if he would fall back into the dream of chasing the ideal image he had of himself.

He would compensate for his experience by over-analyzing his behaviors and the way in which he spoke to others. He was always in a constant state of inner judgement and turmoil. This was all a deflection from the central experience of seeing the insubstantiality of his self-image and avoiding the accompanying shame. I pointed out to Andy how his over-analyzing was another pattern of self-indulgence; it was nothing but personal will and a means of defending against his experience of being a fraud. "You're using one illusion to get rid of another," I told him. The mind can't get rid of the mind. If Andy could accept his state, if he could accept "being a fraud" and the associated shame, this may help him make contact with the truth of his being and become more real in life. Being real meant he could be himself, even if that meant a career change or divorce. This is the risk we all take when we move closer to what is real within us. When we speak the truth and live from truth, it doesn't mean our life is all rainbows and unicorns; it usually means we have to make some very real and difficult life changes.

To invite a deeper acceptance of his situation, I just went for it and asked Andy, "What's the problem in being a fraud?" He looked at me perplexed. I pointed out to Andy that we are all frauds, all of us; we are all in the same boat. "We're all frauds at some point in our lives, in our relationships, at work, in our way of relating in the world. What would it be to accept yourself as a fraud?" "I'm not a fraud though," he explained. I laughed and said, "Are you sure about that? You are trying so desperately to not come off as a fraud that you give off the vibe of being nothing but a fraud. What would it be like to accept this part of you, to accept that you're a fraud and stop judging yourself for it?"

I then invited Andy to say aloud a few times the statement, "Brian, I'm a fraud," but with the caveat of saying it without any judgement or avoidance. He reported feeling shaky and trembling within. He was having a hard time trying to muster the words to say it, and I could sense he was about to collapse within himself (a typical shame-based response). I reminded Andy not to judge his experience but to allow shame to be there. He nodded in agreement, and after a short period of time, he began uttering the words "Brian, I'm a fraud," and after saying it several more times, he straightened himself up in the chair and started to smile. "What do you notice?" I asked. "It's weird," he said, "I don't feel as bad anymore. I feel calmer. I'm a fraud, I'm a fraud!" He laughingly shouted. "Me too, welcome to the club," I replied. We both started laughing together, and it seemed Andy now understood what was being pointed to. He could allow space around being a fraud and did not have to turn it into a problem. By owning his experience, the mind relaxed, and he appeared more into the flow and enjoying his own energy. I invited him to continue embracing his inner fraud from a place of surrender and no judgement throughout the rest of the week and to take note of any insights and transformations. This aided in lessening his shame and living a more authentic life. Working with shame is a critical step in self-realization. By accepting our shame, we move deeper into the empty nature of who we are.

Chapter 2: Freedom From the Rusty Cage of Doubt

If you doubt your Self, the truth of your Self, you will suffer and search for release from this suffering through thought, emotion, and physical circumstance.

- Gangaji

Doubt is a disease of the mind that keeps us stuck in the dream state. It's a reaction of the mind to experiencing the present moment. Now it's perfectly natural, even wise, to doubt our experience; to thoroughly investigate and question what we see, hear, feel, sense and experience, and arrive at our own conclusions, but the doubt I want to speak to here, is the reaction of doubt which ignores and minimizes those experiences that are actually helpful for us in waking up from the dream state. In this way, doubt is used to remain separate and defined, in control and secure. Sadly, when we doubt the truth of our being, we are caged in separation. And lately, I've noticed many people disregarding their experiences; important experiences that would otherwise have been transformative for them in their journey, blowing them off as irrational, mere hallucinations, or ignoring them altogether.

Here, we doubt our spontaneous intuitions, insights, power and creativity, and encounters that fall out of the realm of the familiar. Encased exclusively in the body and mind, we are dragged along the wheel of life and death. Locked in a focal point of self-perception, we are bound to the dualistic life of the self and other, life and death, good and evil, and right and wrong; a linear and dead life. When we do this, we not only limit our full range of human experience, but we continue to live a rigid and wooden life, caged in the limits of believing we are merely a body and mind. Our perception does not expand beyond what we can see and feel with our senses.

It makes sense, though, because since birth, we were taught to only trust and believe what we can experience through our senses. To understand only through our minds, and to doubt everything else which does not fit within our particular belief system or world view. The usual mode of relating to ourselves, our inner experiences, and the world is through our senses. We rely upon them to help make sense of our place in existence. This is the only lens, the only aperture of awareness in which to view life. The danger with this is that it keeps our dream world intact, and anything that challenges or goes beyond our senses is deemed untrustworthy or simply a part of our imagination. This is the typical state of the separate self. Anything which challenges the dream we have built up and maintained is discarded from awareness.

The Integral philosopher, Ken Wilber, called this way of being and living "Flat Land," where the rational world is the only living truth. It is one-dimensional living, lacking fullness, mystery, and vibrancy. I really like this concept because it paints an image of a *dead zone* where there is no room or allowance for our spirit to shine. There is no appreciation, value, or significance given to those experiences that fall outside of the rational mind. Ken

Wilber goes on to describe how we have three modes of knowing and experiencing existence available to us – the eye of flesh, the eye of mind, and the eye of contemplation. The eye of flesh is knowing through our senses, the eye of mind is understanding through mental cognition, and the eye of contemplation is a knowing beyond the mind itself. Awakening is beyond the mind and to only use our senses and cognitive abilities will be limiting since the mind cannot understand that which is beyond itself. So using the first two modes of knowing to understand experiences that are non-ordinary in nature will be deemed irrational and thus insignificant. To appreciate experiences of an awakened kind is to embrace the eye of contemplation.[ix] Embracing the four keys of awakening of surrender, taking no position, grace, and humour, are examples of activating the eye of contemplation, as well as various meditation and contemplative practices.

Breaking Out of the Prison of Doubt

Existence manifests itself in a variety of ways that challenge the rational mind; visions and auditory experiences, psychic phenomenon, sudden insights, feelings of oneness and bliss, synchronistic events, and intuitions, are all ways in which the mind is challenged to give up its throne of separation. The moment we doubt our primordial existence is the moment we disconnect from the truth of our being. This pattern of doubt played a major role in stifling my life and keeping me caged up in a perpetual state of self-protectiveness. I wouldn't allow myself to see three feet ahead of me. It was a theme that dominated my life from a very young age. I would always second guess my actions and decisions, disregard anything that seemed out of the realm of possibility, freeze up when I needed to give a presentation, and doubt what I would see because I didn't understand. As a result, I looked to others to provide me with guidance, support, and validation. I could not trust my own read on things. It was such a debilitating condition for me, and looking back at it now, I saw myself as nothing more than a self-protective shell, void of any real substance. It felt like a death and a form of self-betrayal. I was in a total state of doubt. I doubted my Being.

However, several years ago, during a particularly difficult time in my life and when my wife was living with brain cancer, there was an experience I could not deny, which opened me up to deeper dimensions of my being. The event blew me open. While sleeping one night, I had a dream of myself and my wife sitting in a dimly lit room with soft green and yellow lighting. We were both sitting beside each other in old chairs, and I could barely see her. In front of us sat an extremely tall man, an abnormally tall man with a magnificent presence about him. We started communicating with each other but not through speech. It seemed like we were speaking to one another through a type of telekinesis. It was the oddest thing. He would simply look at me, and I could hear his thoughts in my mind. He appeared earnest in his communication with me, and I immediately felt the importance of his words. My wife sat there looking at me as if she knew what was being shared with me and the importance of it, and I sensed her supportive energy. As I became more aware and focused on the encounter, I could finally "hear" what was being said. "Build a bridge, and the heart will cross it," he said. In the dream, I asked, "Who are you?" "Osiris," he replied.

I woke up instantly knowing something important had happened to me. Something of significance was revealed to me. There was a qualitative difference in this experience compared to other non-ordinary events I have encountered. I believe, due to my wife's health concerns, I was open and receptive and, therefore, couldn't deny it. I knew enough to pay attention to this. My being was craving support and understanding. So I quickly wrote down what I had experienced. I had no idea who this Osiris figure was or what this encounter meant to me, but I knew enough to record it. The absence of doubt allowed me the opportunity to integrate my experience. There was a message here for me, and I needed to understand it at a deep level. Rather than using the mind to figure it all out, I needed to let it reveal itself to me. I researched the name Osiris, and I was surprised, shocked even, to learn he was the Egyptian God of death. His visitation and message mirrored what I was dealing with in my waking state. The message of "building a bridge and allowing the heart to cross it" began to unfold and reveal its meaning – I was invited to surrender to the process of death, not to fight it, and not to see death as a problem.

Death was only a problem to the body and mind, not to the truth of who we are. The heart represented love, that which can never die. The arrow hit its mark. I heard the message, the invitation with my whole being, and I felt my heart expand. I felt like a container of experience holding everything that was happening in my life at that time; not as an individual self but as an impersonal presence and the heart of existence as such. The power and richness of the message were unmistakable. The hugeness of this teaching would continue to manifest and reveal its truth throughout the rest of our life together, allowing me to become much more able to welcome the unknown and not react to it in my usual ways. To wake up out of doubt is to trust our true nature.

Chapter 3: Buried in the Graveyard of Desire

All suffering is born of desire.

- Nisargaddatta Maharaj

Waking up does not guarantee that all of our old self-management strategies have been dealt with, and desire is one such self-management strategy. To be buried in the graveyard of desire is to be buried under the weight of the illusion that something external to ourselves will bring us wholeness. This exists in the pursuit of drugs, alcohol, relationships, food, work, sex and love, spirituality, and the idea of Enlightenment. We think once we fulfill our desires, we will gain everlasting happiness but only to find ourselves repeatedly disappointed. Once we grab hold of it and believe it will deliver us the goods, we end up as twisted beings, stunted and haunted, endlessly seeking to feed an insatiable beast. A beast of our own making. Desire then rules our whole life; our being is tangled up in false promises and distorted beliefs where we are never satisfied. It all leads to a massive state of confusion and chaos where we are pulled this way and that, controlled by an energetic force of our own making. The fire of desire burns as we have built a lengthy history with it through time. It burns up our connection to being and our essence, shutting down our heart and cutting us off from our own wisdom, understandings, and presence of the moment. It is a state of mindlessness really. We are like a zombie, wandering around aimlessly seeking to fill ourselves, to experience and consume whatever is in front of us. We end up trapped in eternity chasing desire, and around and around we go, caught in a loop of our own making.

Now, don't get me wrong, we all have desires of some sort or another, like the desire to go on a weekend trip, to spend time with friends and family, or the desire for a meatball sandwich. But the desire I'm pointing to here is the longing for something outside ourselves, thinking it will ultimately complete and fulfill us. There is a vast difference between desiring a coffee in the morning to wanting a coffee in the morning to make me feel whole and complete. The energy behind this type of wanting is what keeps us stuck in the dream state and makes us a slave to the mind and desire. This type of need indicates a sense of incompleteness and the inability to be within the present moment. There is the perception that the present moment is not okay as it is, and with this, the origin of suffering begins. At the heart of desire is the inability to be in this moment. This moment is not enough. There is something wrong or missing in this instance. It's not complete, it's too painful, or it's too boring. This moment needs to be different then from what it is. The demand that things have to be better is the beginning of chaos. Our demands of the moment are another way of saying "no" to existence.

> *Desiring never satisfies because it is an unreal experience. It doesn't have the realness or solidity of truth because desiring is not oriented in the present moment. The object of desire is always something that is not present in the moment (it doesn't make sense to desire something that is already here). A desire is always concerned with the past of the future, and no fantasy of the past or future will ever satisfy.*[x]

You may have noticed this in your own life where you felt the desire for something so strongly that you just needed to have it; a desire so powerful that without it, you felt incomplete. If you are in recovery, it may have been that next drink or cigarette, or it's the long hours immersed at work, or food, or the next relationship hook-up. Not getting the fix can place one in a dangerous situation. It can lead to ill health, suffering, or even loss of life. This can be seen within the addictions' community. The power we have projected onto our object of wanting consumes us. At some point, we have to get to the root of desire and see how it is being fed. It's not enough to simply change our behaviors or casually manipulate our situation too. We have to get to the bottom of our dilemma and see what it is we are doing to ourselves. How is it that we are selling out our true nature for an illusion? How is it that having glimpsed my True Nature, I continue to get lost in desire? In what ways do we strengthen the energy of desire? Just see where this has been the case in your own life. If we really slow ourselves down and investigate our yearnings, we will not only notice the mind is nothing but a factory of desires, a production line of greed and lust, but that it is in the attention and fixation we give desire which ultimately creates our suffering. This is an important insight, as desire will always be there, but it is our fixation on it that matters. It's the energy-attention behind it that is critical to look at.

Brian Theriault

Sitting in the Fire of Desire

Desire is habit energy. The invitation is to relax our attention and sit in the fire of longing without moving. I remember working with a client, Ian, a few years back, who, when sitting in the urge of desire, could see in his mind's eye the image of hundreds of outstretched hands extending from his body and grabbing at objects of desire. Each arm had a different level of energy and colour to them, depending on how much lusting was associated with each object. The stronger the desire, the brighter the arm. He could also witness the birth of new desires, seeing them as finger-like parturitions slowly growing from within his body. Little fingers, already reaching to be satisfied. When he was asked to watch each arm of desire without following through on its demands to be satisfied and to simply observe it, the color and energetic charge of each arm would start to diminish in intensity until dissolving completely. He felt quite disturbed by this, but he saw how desire operated within himself, and more importantly, he saw how he fed it and how he could free himself from it. As he began to relax though, the energetic charge of desire began to loosen, and he arrived at the opportunity to really see through it. He landed in a change of perception from that of perceiving as the mind to that of perceiving prior to the mind.

We need to allow ourselves to be consumed by the energetic force of it, without managing, defending, or feeding it. We have to burn it through. We must allow the fire of desire to burn itself out. If we fight desire we feed it and give it more energy and power. Our thoughts and fantasies about desire are the kindling. Relax the temptation to fuel it and relax beyond craving itself. This can be excruciatingly painful because the mind's natural tendency is to fulfill desire, so it will scream out in agony when there is no follow-through. No follow-through is the death of the mind.

As we sit in the fire of desire, we fall deeper into the moment; we are the moment, and there is no distance or demand on it. Life takes on a whole new different quality. We start to vibrate at a deeper level of being, where life becomes rich and full and, we wonder why we sold out for illusionary crumbs. Freed from fixating on desire, we disappear more and more into the mystery of existence, not knowing and not desiring. We live now, in this moment, the raw reality of *just this*. We are complete *now*.

In the course of one's transformational journey, it becomes essential that the lie of desire is exposed. It's imperative one becomes aware of the false nature of desire. Desire leads us further away from the present moment, from being happy and blissful right now. This moment is truth, but the mind can't handle it, so it manifests endless carrots of wishes to chase in order to grant the illusion of getting somewhere and feeling satisfied. Wanting can never lead us to the truth. It's in the absence of following through on those aspirations that we think will complete us which brings us right back to what is already complete in the present moment.

Chapter 4: Fornicating Towards Wholeness: Transforming Sex Addiction

Sun, sun, sun
Burn, burn, burn
Moon, moon, moon
I will get you soon...soon...soon!
I am the Lizard King
I can do anything.

- Jim Morrison

Desire can be intense. Mystical poet, rock star, or *Shaman*, Jim Morrison orchestrated a symphony of dark and seductive energies that captivated audiences worldwide during the rock and roll scene of the late 1960s and early 1970s. For Jim, the mythical "Lizard King" appeared to represent his *daimen* or alter ego, whereby he flourished in the realms of unconventional living. The energy of the "Lizard King" was seductive, mysterious and magnetic, thriving in situations where fear and danger were always present. It was about pushing the limits of conventional boundaries even at the cost of his close relationships, suffering legal implications and personal health.[xi]

Whether it was exposing himself on stage or delighting in personalizing the Oedipesian paradox while his mother was attending one of his concerts, nothing was off-limits for Jim. He was a *Shaman* and trickster and personified sex, drugs, and rock n' roll. Tragically, all myths have an expiry date, and perhaps for Jim, it was the belief in his own myth of "I am the Lizard King, I can do anything" that brought about his early demise. The hard and fast lifestyle of sex, drugs, and rock n' roll has claimed many musicians but, for some, this lifestyle can morph into an opportunity of profound surrender and personal transformation. This was the case with Jack, someone I had the opportunity to work with therapeutically for over a year.

I have worked with many musicians over the years, and for Jack, a young man in his thirties, the rock and roll lifestyle of Jim Morrison mirrored his own life in many ways. The belief in his own myth of a "sexualized guitar rock god" was beginning to wreak havoc on his personal and professional life, which led him to seek therapy. Jack was a musician who played lead guitar in a rock band for several years. He lived the dream, and although he conquered the demons of drugs and alcohol through his involvement with Refuge Recovery support groups and Buddhist practices, his sexual acting-out behavior continued unabated. His wife finally had enough of his compulsive affairs and his many nameless one-night stands and threatened to file for divorce if he did not change his ways. His band was beginning to question his commitments due to his frequent absenteeism from jam sessions and recent lack of production at concerts. They were considering letting him go.

The existential crisis of the possibility of losing his marriage, and band became the catalyst for Jack to finally explore his sexual compulsivity. During our initial consultation session, Jack revealed that a lot of his acting-out behavior was intertwined with his stage-like persona of "guitar rock god," whereby, while performing, he felt omnipotent and able to live on the edge, scanning the audience for the next sexual encounter. Although uniquely his own, his pain echoed the vast majority of clients I have worked with struggling to climb out of the trenches of sexual addiction. The searing pain and shame of living a lie, manipulation and deceit, shattered relationships, inauthentic connections with others and the world, and profound isolation, are all too common themes in a sex addict's life.

The Rise and Fall of the "Master of the Universe"

In my practice, many people struggling with sex addiction, coupled with the need to address the desire energy associated with it, need to confront the narcissistic personality structure. Patrick Carnes, a leading figure in the treatment of sex addiction, coined the term "Masters of the Universe" when describing sex addicts:

> *The Master of the Universe theme emerges in addict's lives in many different ways. But constant is the rationale that all is justified because of the addict's uniqueness, specialness, or superiority. In their addiction, they are set apart from others, either made of 'the right stuff' or having some special right or need others don't have. Being out of control requires that you have no limits. Overextension, denial, sexual acting out, trouble, and unmanageability mingle in the addicts who live on the edge.[xii]*

The master of the universe craves specialness, uniqueness, and mirroring from wherever and from whoever he can get it from. They believe they are God, omnipotent, and all-powerful, possessing the belief that they are the most brilliant, charismatic, and totally irresistible. They also possess unrealistic beliefs about what they can do, who they can be, and what they can accomplish in life. The narcissism runs deep. The need to be seen and mirrored is fuel for the master of the universe. The sex addict's whole identity is dependent upon being sexually mirrored, whether it's through the next nameless sexual encounter or through engaging in psychological fantasy, the need is great. One has identified with a severely distorted self-image of themselves, one that is weak and flimsy and where their sense of wholeness is tied up in the next sexual encounter. One can never truly be themselves because they are living a lie. They are in love with a self-image, and they will go to great lengths to defend it. Many people I work with, report to me that without the sexual mirroring of their identity, how they see themselves begins to dissolve, revealing pain and an underlying sense of incompleteness. The incompleteness then leads to unbearable pain, which is too painful to be with, and so the need for another sexual encounter begins as a means of managing the pain and shoring up one's identity. Here, we see the cycle of sex addiction playing itself out.

The master of the universe lurks everywhere, even within spiritual communities. Far too many spiritual teachers have gone on to have affairs with their students and acted out inappropriately. Some believed themselves to be so unique and spiritually enlightened as to have special powers, which would prevent them from giving or even contracting sexually transmitted diseases. The mind uses spiritual truths as a means of serving itself, inflating one's sense of self to maintain control, security, and a perceived sense of specialness. Even with a deep awakening experience, there can continue to be traces of unresolved fixations and distorted self-images which need to be worked through. Again, this is due to the need to be seen and appreciated in a particular way. The problem lies again in identifying with a lie, a delusion, a veil of sorts that has no substance, and is not a direct experience of one's true being. It's all a façade, and underneath this front lies a deep and searing pain, not only of the unresolved pains and personal traumas accumulated over a lifetime but of the fear of an underlying emptiness: the fear of a nothingness percolating at the depths of one's being.

The experience of nothingness is a direct threat to one's self-image; it usurps one's false sense of self and personal control in the world. The lie of separateness is illuminated. Instead of reacting out of nothingness by engaging in the cycle of addiction, if one can stay with the experience of nothingness and see the truth of their situation when one realizes they have been living a lie, then the work of self-realization can begin. Like with all types of addictions, it's when the addict hits rock bottom that the opportunity for transformation can take place. When one has fallen to their knees and surrendered, realizing they can't live the way they have been all these years, is when we do first see a real potential of self-discovery. I have found the diamond approach of self-realization to be a direct method in dismantling the master of the universe personality.

Using the "Diamond Approach" in Transforming the "Master of the Universe"

The Diamond Approach identifies narcissism as the main barrier to self-realization and offers a working-through process of undercutting this obstacle via levels of self-inquiry. It is an unfolding stage-like process with 18 identifiable steps of transformation. Each step represents a significant action in the integration of one's personality into nondual being. I will explore five of these essential steps as they relate to deconstructing the identity of a sex addict. They include: 1. The empty shell and fakeness, 2. The narcissistic wound and rage, 3. The great betrayal, 4. Ego activity, and 5. The great chasm and black space. So before we return to the case of Jack, let's briefly look at these five steps.[xiii]

Exposing the empty shell of the sex addict is a critical first step in awakening into *nondual being*. Lies, deceit, manipulation, and control are just some aspects that keep the master of the universe personality in place. This persona structure is likened to that of an empty shell because without the sexualized mirroring, it begins to thin out and dissolve.

> *He begins to realize that what he has been taking to be himself is actually a shell, devoid of any substantial reality or inherent richness ... The empty shell feels impoverished, insubstantial, and false. He feels hollow and vacant, as if his body has become a shell of tension with its insides sucked out of it.*[xiv]

This is the lie of identification. Through a process of surrender, the hollow shell of the master of the universe personality is exposed. This is often seen in sex addicts who experience a profound existential crisis in their lives, commonly referred to as "hitting rock bottom." For many reaching this point, it starts to become clear that life has been lived as a lie, and to continue doing so would not only lead to deeper despair but to the possibility of death. The task here is not to defend against this familiarity but to allow it in its entirety. As one ceases to resurrect the empty shell through continued acting out, one gains distance on the addictive behavior and falls further into the deeper recesses of their being. One begins to experience truth.

However, as the empty shell is exposed, an underlying pain emerges. The pain here is intense, and one sees, perhaps for the first time, just how much of their life and energy had been spent in supporting a façade. It is a crisis of being, which accounts for one of the reasons why I hear many addicts relapsing in the first year of recovery. As the sex addict disengages from the need for sexual mirroring, the resulting crisis of being can slowly be tolerated. The inherent rage is a reaction to the wound of having lived a lie and can be seen in the addict who self-sabotages their recovery through projection and blame. But attempting to bypass this wound simply prolongs the suffering. The only remedy is to accept, surrender, understand, and go through the pain, to step into the eye of it without the desire for escape and to allow it. As a person goes through the pain and rage, the feeling of self-betrayal emerges fully.

We see that we betrayed ourselves, just as the people in our environment betrayed us. We chose their company and approval over Essence. We recognize that this betrayal is the deeper one, at the very roots of our disconnection from our essential nature. We feel the hurt now as more terrible, the wound a bottomless abyss of pain. There is great sorrow, regret, and sometimes shame, guilt, and self-hatred.[xv]

Here, the question I will typically ask clients is, "At what point did you say to yourself that sex was the answer for you?" This type of inquiry helps snap the habitual tendency to project and blame others for their situation. One has to see how they chose the world of sex addiction over truth. Doing so allows one's awareness to penetrate to the core of their being in the here and now moment. It is only in the eternal present moment that the vast silent nature of who we are can be revealed.

In response to the realization of self-betrayal and emerging experience of emptiness, the mind will raise hell in the form of frantic ego activity, including forms of chronic self-obsessiveness, the need for self-assurances, and self-recognition. Although this type of activity can occur at any stage of unfolding and self-realization, it is intense here because the underlying void is perceived directly and understood as a threat. One may try to defend against the emptiness by reverting back to the old addictive behaviors that are seen as having lesser consequences. This can be observed in the sex addict who has given up voyeuristic acting-out but has engaged in "lesser" behaviors such as internet pornography. A great deal of my work here consists of inviting people to not react from the emerging stillness and hollowness of their being, to not judge it as a terrible thing, and relax into it. The judgement towards it is what leads to relapse.

As ego activity ceases, it becomes easier to abide in the emptiness and to relax into the great chasm of being. Falling into the chasm reveals that all of one's reactions and associated feelings toward the experience of nothingness have been that of the separate self, which has now been seen as none other than an illusion. The knot of self-identity unravels much more, allowing one to descend further and further into the vast spaciousness of being. While descending further, the black empty stillness becomes clearer, and incredibly, the realization is that it is none other than one's self. One has always been this black, spacious emptiness from which all identifications arise.

In the black space we are aware of the absence of the sense of self… it is a nothingness, but it is a nothingness that is rich, that is satisfying precisely because of its emptiness. It is a direct sense of endless stillness, of pure peacefulness, of an infinity of blackness that is radiant because of its purity. This is not the experience of a self, an observer beholding the endlessness of space; rather, it is the experience of the self experiencing itself as the infinity of peaceful space.[xvi]

Now let's return to Jack, who we discussed earlier, and see how elements of the diamond approach were used in working through his narcissism. Jack had read over the material I gave him in our consultation session, and he called me a week later to schedule a counselling appointment. Although there were concepts he did not understand, particularly the impersonal aspects of consciousness, he was interested in the approach and open to applying it in his life.

Exposing the Empty Shell and Fakeness

Jack arrived at our second session appearing heavy and defeated. His agony and desperation energetically filled the room. His pain was real and his plea for help was sincere. He seemed caught up in his mind and projected worst-case scenarios of the future. He had a lot to lose if he continued his ways. We took some time to acknowledge his thoughts and feelings while I also pointed out to him, although he was indeed on the edge of losing his marriage if he continued his behaviors, none of his worst-case scenarios had occurred, and he had an opportunity to transform his ways. Jack slowed down, appearing more open and less identified with his mind.

It was clear that a large part of Jack's identity had been tied into being a "sexualized rock god." It was important to deconstruct this myth and bring out the addictive personality by allowing it uncensored space within our counselling session, where it could be seen and understood. Fighting the addictive persona through cognitive reframing was Jack's typical position, and he did find some temporary relief in that. However, it seemed hopeless, as the addictive cycle would continue. Instead of fighting it, I invited Jack to "bring it in the room" and allow it "free reign" as a means of understanding it. Revealing what the addictive personality was chasing, and more importantly, what it was avoiding in the present moment was crucial. We explored this through an experimental exercise adopted from psychologists John Firman and Ann Gila. Individuals were asked to imagine themselves in a situation where they could feel the urge to act out their addiction. However, instead of following through with it, they were encouraged to sit with the pressing urge and get to the bottom of what was fueling it. The flip side of this exercise is in inviting one to imagine themself to be back in the exact moment where they are about to act out their addiction, and instead of withholding their urge, one is allowed to experience it fully, to experience the addictive behavior in its entirety.[xvii]

I first invited Jack to imagine himself acting out his addictive behavior, to fully engage his stage persona of "guitar rock god." As he did this, he smiled, sharing that he felt "electric" and "totally out there and alive." He recalled many situations while performing on stage where he would scan the audience for his next sexual encounter and have his "roadies" (stagehands) bring the person back to the VIP area. He reported feeling an abundance of energy racing throughout his body. Jack was beginning to notice that the feelings of "aliveness" and "being in control" were elements that fuelled his addictive behavior. We took some time to process his experience. I then followed up with a guided imagery exercise where I asked him to imagine himself standing in an arena with tens of thousands of other musicians playing out the same rock god myth he was playing. I invited him to see himself in the company of thousands of rock stars playing out the same pattern of getting noticed and chasing the next sexual encounter. After some time, Jack looked puzzled, as he noticed the energy dissipating from his body. He said, "I feel flat. Like I don't have the stage." He seemed lost. Since a majority of his energy and awareness was fixated on his sexualized rock star myth, it was no surprise to see him lost and energetically deflated. He wasn't all that special and unique. This appeared to give Jack a significant glimpse into the empty nature of his self-image, where he was able to see the compulsion of his personality as an empty shell fed through sexualized mirroring.

Jack was now tapping into the underbelly of his addictive behavior. For the second part of the exercise, Jack observed that underneath his addictive urge was tremendous fear and panic, which manifested in his chest and belly. While staying with his experience, I invited him to inquire further into this by asking, "What is the worst of that? What is the worst thing about experiencing fear?" He replied, "I feel like I would be swallowed up and I would go crazy." "And the worst of that is?" I asked. "My fear, I think, is that I would disappear." "And the worst of that?" I continued. "Well, I wouldn't be here," he said. Jack appeared somewhat shocked at what he had just discovered and was slowly making connections to how much of what he took himself to be was fake; how much of his self-preoccupation was used in avoiding the feeling of non-existence.

Although we would revisit this theme in further sessions, Jack was starting to glimpse the inherent "fakeness" of his self-image. To build on this momentum, I instructed him to practice using the above-guided imagery exercise at home to help free up his fixated awareness and bound-up energy.

The Narcissistic Wound and Rage

It was towards our seventh session that Jack was able to open up more to the underlying pain fueling his compulsive search. He was finding it difficult to give it all up. Jack garnered a considerable amount of mirroring mileage out of his guitar rock myth, so his difficulties made sense. Each sexual encounter reinforced a sense of uniqueness and feelings of power and control. As he was making some progress in dis-identifying from the self-image, he was able to make contact with the pain deep within his being. Interestingly, while exploring his pain further, he made the connection to how it would intensify when he felt "overlooked" by a potential sexual encounter who favored the lead singer or another member of the band. For example, Jack recalled a situation while partying with his band and several female guests after a performance, where he was reacting out of anger and rage when the lead singer was showered with accolades and praise for performing energetically that night and singing powerful songs. Jack remembered feeling "dismissed and small" and countered "passive-aggressively" by interrupting the bond and screaming that if it wasn't for his memorable power cords and guitar hooks, he (the lead singer) wouldn't have anything to gyrate too. Although Jack smiled when recalling this, he went on to share how things escalated afterwards, having returned to his hotel room, and in a fit of rage, trashed the whole place.

In making these correlations, Jack noticed his belly would contract and tighten up as a means of protection and resistance. A large part of his work here was to sit in the pain without any commentary or reaction. This proved extraordinarily difficult for him since the habitual reaction to escape from his pain had been built up over a lifetime. Instead of suggesting he shore up a more positive sense of self to compensate for the wound, as traditional recovery approaches would suggest, I simply invited Jack to allow the pain to be there. Compensating for the pain reinforces another self-image, whereas having an open curiosity towards it, may reveal the illusionary nature of the addictive personality. An important intervention here, was for Jack to practice at home for as much as he could, sitting in his pain without any judgement towards it, any need to change or add to it, or even trying to heal it. He was to sit in the eye of his pain without any movement for or against it without redefining himself through a reaction. The hope was that by cultivating non-judgemental awareness, Jack would be able to tolerate the pain enough, which would aid in exposing the emptiness of his whole sexualized rock-star myth.

The Great Betrayal

It was in our thirteenth session when we explored the theme of self-betrayal. Initially, as we continued processing the narcissistic wound and associated feelings of worthlessness and pain, he connected these feelings to traumatizing experiences while growing up. As a teenager, he recalled situations of verbal and emotional abuse at the hands of his stepfather. His mother was a non-protecting bystander, which resulted in feelings of abandonment. It was Jack's belief that his sexual acting-out was a reaction to his stepfather's abuse. He felt traumatized and betrayed by his primary caregivers. What appeared to be created here was the victim-perpetrator cycle. His sexual performance was indeed a part of his coping mechanism from the abuse he received, except it did not acknowledge the important piece of self-betrayal.

An important aspect of deconstructing his addictive personality was to dissolve the victim-perpetrator cycle through owning and taking some responsibility for having sold out his being in favor of being sexually mirrored by others. This was difficult for Jack because a lot of his awareness was locked into being victimized. This became a delicate process, as Jack could view the invitation of taking some responsibility for having sold out his true nature as a means of minimizing the abuse he experienced, causing him to see me, the therapist, as expressing a lack of attunement, compassion, and support. We moved back and forth, acknowledging and resolving his personal trauma while also ensuring that Jack was taking ownership of his self-betrayal. It meant tracking down the moment he consciously chose to identify sexual acting-out as the answer to resolving his pain. Jack reflected on this for some time and saw it was somewhere in his late teens and early twenties, while playing guitar in garage bands and performing at small clubs and where he received a lot of sexual attention, that his acting-out really took off. He noticed it was in his late twenties when playing guitar had shifted gears from pure enjoyment and creativity to being used in facilitating the next sexual encounter. Here, he was beginning to see the deeper nature of his own self-betrayal. This opened Jack up further in liberating himself from the narcissism of his addictive personality and in taking responsibility for where he places his awareness in each and every moment.

Ego Activity

Naturally, a consistent theme that emerged throughout the majority of our sessions together, was the frantic flurry of ego activity. A mind field of constant distractions, avoidance patterns, rationalizations, desires, and justifications were employed to shore up a familiar sense of self. And, as we have learned, a master of the universe is not so willing to give up the throne of specialness. The dissolution of Jack's glorified self-image was increasing and so were the mind's defensive strategies. As the mirroring supports of the habitual sexual encounters cease, the addictive persona will perceive this as a psychic death.

Although Jack reported some success in not acting out sexually over the course of our work together, he observed how his compulsive personality would find various ways of reasserting itself. For instance, he recalled that while enjoying a night out with his wife at a popular club, he would finesse his way into being waited upon by the most attractive bar hostess or lock eyes with women who were dancing. Tears welled up as he described this activity. "I couldn't even allow myself to enjoy our time together. It was all about getting an 'energy buzz.' I wanted to see if I could 'hook up' without my wife catching me. How crazy is that?!" By being mirrored by the perceived most attractive person, it shored up his sense of specialness.

A useful intervention here was in instructing Jack to practice observing his desired fixations from the spaciousness prior to his mind. Ordinarily, one's awareness is always moving forward in time and fixating itself on particular objects, thoughts, people and emotions, thus limiting the amount of recognition available for the present moment. For Jack, the invitation became about pulling his consciousness back prior to having an impression, fantasy, preference, desire, or knowledge of a particular person, revealing the empty spaciousness of pure awareness. Observing his surroundings from "back there" would hopefully allow Jack to be present and less prone to being pulled by his egoic desires. Although difficult at first, he would report in later sessions having a marked ability in cutting off his projected desires and noticed an increased amount of energy available in the present moment.

The Great Chasm and Black Space

The more Jack was able to see through his self-image of a sexualized rock star, the more distance he was able to get from habitually acting it out. He would arrive at some of our sessions, sharing that he experienced an increase in his energy and contributions to his band and loving connections with his family. Freeing up his awareness meant an increase in understanding of the emptiness at the core of his being. However, Jack felt fearful around this experience, fearful of going crazy and being out of control. The states of emptiness he felt in his meditation practice did not compare to the depth of *Emptiness* he was experiencing now, having unpacked the master of the universe personality. Meditation alone won't clear up all our patterns, confusions, and fixations; we must confront ourselves in a real and genuine way. The mind will avoid this experience at all costs. A fall into the chasm of being is the death of the mind. Here, I pointed out to Jack I suspected his fear of "going crazy" was a story he continually told himself, which warded off the experience of emptiness in the *now* moment. Letting go of our stories and judgements opens one up to the vast *Emptiness*.

I could sense Jack's fear slowly building in intensity. He was looking a little shaky and appeared to be searching for a psychological escape. Rather than align with his defensive tactics, I viewed this as a moment of opportunity; I wanted to see if Jack could take the plunge into nondual being here and now. I asked him, "Can you see that this moment is it? Can you let go totally, right here and now?" Jack was wide-eyed and seemed to struggle with this experience. I then followed up with, "What would happen if you just stopped fighting your experience?" After a few moments, Jack let out a deep exhalation and seemed to relax more into the moment. "I've been fighting this all my life," he realized. I nodded in reply and invited him to notice that "Nothing, not even the desire for sex, can save you here. We have to let it all go, all of our self-imposed strategies of escaping the void."

Jack allowed my invitational statement to sink in. He appeared to relax even more and made a shift from a state of tension to a *fall-into the present moment* one. "There's no 'little me' here," he said, pointing to his forehead. I smiled in response. From here, Jack also realized the absence of any addictive desire or need to be validated. He reported feeling open, spacious, and non-reactive. He felt free from the habitual contraction of the separate self. As a means of celebrating this breakthrough, we sat in silence for a little while without the need to say or do anything at all.

The task, now, for Jack, was to abide in nondual being from moment to moment and within all aspects of his life. It was for him to be free of the chains of self-identification and merge with the empty stillness of existence, without the need to be mirrored or validated in any defining way. It was a gift to embrace the nondual journey with Jack, and I often wonder how he lives his life now and what realizations he has experienced along the way of continued self-discovery.

Chapter 5: Waking Up Out of the Black Hole of Trauma

For twenty years I was in turmoil
Seething and angry, but now my time has come!
The crow laughs, an arhat emerges from the filth,
And in the sunlight a jade beauty sings!

- Zen Master Ikkyu

While curled up in the middle of the circle in the group room, my chest tightened up like a vice grip with tremendous fear and terror racing throughout my body. The fear was intense. There was an image of myself descending to the bottom of the ocean, waving and thrashing about. I thought I was going to die. Here, I was invited to surrender and cooperate with the process, to be with the intensity of the experience but from a place of no judgement. Confused, I took the risk to do just that; however, I would bounce in and out of fear, and as a result, I was continually reminded not to judge the process and see that this moment is it. And then, suddenly, in the midst of my internal chaos, there was no division; I felt merged with the pain that was arising in my body and mind. An awesome black stillness revealed itself; a silence so great echoed throughout my Being. I was none other than this black calm. Here, I felt I did not exist, and yet, at the same time, I was very much aware of the entire process taking place. The chaotic energy ran its course and finally thinned out to reveal a deep sense of peace and relaxation.

As previously mentioned in my invitation, the above experience took place well over fifteen years ago while completing an undergraduate degree in Addictions Counselling. It was my first direct experience of nondual consciousness and subsequently facilitated a psycho-spiritual journey towards wholeness. It would be several years later before I would come to fully appreciate and understand what actually took place. For many years, I had avoided the pain of my biographical history, with the traumatic imprints collected over the course of my then, short life. Of course, at the time, I did not have the language or understanding of what took place within that profound group experience, but the event was so incredibly shocking that it radically changed the course of my life, and essentially my work with counselling clients experiencing trauma.

In both the Buddhist and Taoist traditions, they name four experiences that can lead to awakening – prolonged meditation, sex, the experience of death, and trauma. If worked with from the lens of awakening, trauma can lead to profound surrender and to the truth of one's being. From the state of absolute surrender, a person can begin to encounter themselves in a way they have never done before. When surrendered and without judgement, an individual's trauma can be addressed and ultimately resolved. Now, I'm not suggesting that by simply surrendering to one's experiences it will miraculously resolve any and all of one's accumulated trauma. However, what I am attempting to point to is another perspective of how, in conjunction with many other trauma treatment approaches, it can be healed in the light of an awakened being. Trauma can open us up to the truth. The spiritual teacher, Jeff Foster, shares on the possibility of this:

> Even the most intense suffering is pointing to the absence of the one who suffers. At the heart of the most intense suffering, right at the heart of it, there is simply nobody there who suffers. Even suffering is pointing to the absence of the separate solid person ... There is pain, but there's nobody there who is in pain. That's the dream, that's the suffering: that there is a person here.[xviii]

This can be seen in descriptive accounts of individuals who suddenly wake up in the eye of their own pain and realize the absence of the self. I loved reading about Eckhart Tolle's description of waking up out of his own trauma of self-separateness. Up until his thirtieth year, he felt as though he lived in a constant state of anxiety, depression, and intrusive thoughts of suicide:

> 'I cannot live with myself any longer.' This was the thought that kept repeating itself in my mind. Then suddenly I became aware of what a peculiar thought it was. 'Am I one or two? If I cannot live with myself, there must be two of me: the 'I' and the 'self' that 'I' cannot live with.' 'Maybe,' I thought, 'only one of them is real.' I was so stunned by this strange realization that my mind stopped. I was fully conscious, but there were no more thoughts ... Without any thought, I felt, I knew, that there is infinitely more to light than we realize ... Everything was fresh and pristine, as if it had just come into existence ... For the next five months, I lived in a state of uninterrupted deep peace and bliss.[xix]

Similarly, Byron Katie experienced a ten-year period spiralling down the vortex of rage, paranoia, and despair, and one morning, while lying on the floor of her room, she woke up to her true nature:

> *All my rage, all the thoughts that had been troubling me, my whole world, the whole world, was gone. At the same time, laughter welled up from the depths and just poured out. Everything was unrecognizable. It was as if something else had woken up. It opened its eyes. It was looking through Katie's eyes. And it was so delightful! It was intoxicated with joy. There was nothing separate, nothing unacceptable to it; everything was its very own self.*[xx]

Even with such a profound opening to our true nature in the midst of trauma, abiding in our natural state isn't so easy. Like most, I found myself wrapped back up in the mind, the idea of separation, and having to revisit unresolved traumas. In doing so, I had to re-realize some important truths and insights that kept my trauma in place. There were two key insights which proved transformational for me – fear is not a problem to be solved and embracing the wisdom of no escape.

Fear is Not a Problem to Be Solved

My first insight into waking up out of trauma was in relation to the energy of fear. Fear was the glue that held my trauma in place. There was an "I" experiencing fear; there was an "I" which trembled in fear and that was frozen in paralysis. I viewed fear as a problem and resolved to get rid of it. Yet, within my frantic attempts to overcome it, I found myself stalled and feeling emotionally crippled. I tackled fear, fought through my trauma, and wrestled with it through many meditative and therapeutic strategies; I tried to transcend it, heal it, reframe it, and work it out physiologically and through catharsis, which provided me with temporary relief and healing. Nevertheless, it would not be long before I found myself back in a state of despair. There was very little joy and celebration in my life. The problem was that I was viewing fear from the wrong perspective. *'What if I just stopped fighting with fear altogether?*' I thought to myself. I had read many insights related to this and opted to try it, so I relaxed all of my tendencies to manage fear, and quite surprisingly, I noticed a transformative quality of stillness and ease. By relaxing into the energy of fear and seeing it as an appropriate response in the moment, I began to feel the free-flowing nature of existence racing throughout my body again. Managing fear rather than feeling fear itself was the problem. The separate self was the barrier. When met head on and without manipulation, fear naturally transforms itself miraculously:

When there is an openness to fear, where can it be found? What a strange creature fear is. It exists only when there is resistance to its existence! When you stop and open to what you have resisted throughout time, you find that fear is not fear. Fear is energy. Fear is space. Fear is the Buddha.[xxi]

The more life is allowed to unfold and reveal itself as it is, without reacting out of our emotions or resisting our states of consciousness, the more one can give up control, trust, and relax in the aliveness of the unknown. Fear becomes an invitation to notice what is already awake and true within ourselves.

The Wisdom of No Escape

Following the wisdom of being with fear in an undefended way is the need to embrace the wisdom of no escape. Embracing the wisdom of no escape was the second insight for me in waking up out of trauma. The spiritual teacher, Karl Renz, gives a personal account of this in his own awakening process while gripped by the story of Yuddhistra and Krishna playing on his television. The story centres upon the aftermath of a bloody battle and the death of Yuddhistra. Upon his death, Yuddhistra saw his loved ones burning in hellfire and suffering eternally. At this moment, Yuddhistra fell into total despair, and the poignant question was asked by Krishna of whether or not he could remain in that condition forever:

> By this time, I was so deeply involved in the play and so completely identified with Yuddhistra that I felt the question was actually addressed to me. He, or I, answered, 'I have no desire to change anything or to avoid pain or suffering. If I must remain in this condition for the remainder of my existence, so be it' ... at this moment an explosion-like experience tore through the back of my head, filling my perception with pure light. At this moment, there was an absolute acceptance of being. Time stopped, ... and the world disappeared, and a kind of pure Is-ness in a glaring light appeared. It was a pulsating silence, and absolute aliveness that was perfect in itself – and I was that.[xxii]

The usual tactic is to run from pain, but when staying in the pain and suffering, the opportunity to awaken exists. Again, we can see the paradoxical nature of healing pain and waking up out of trauma. Every moment is seen as a chance to awaken, and therefore, there is no need to escape our situation. We surrender to existence. This is the recognition that no escape is possible or needed. We don't ignore life; we don't make a problem out of the states we happen to find ourselves in, and we embrace whatever is unfolding for us in a clear and open way.

Mark's Journey

Mark contacted me wishing to do trauma resolution work to "heal the demons from the past," he said. In our first session, he reported feeling continually haunted by his past traumas like the abuse he suffered from his family, particularly from his father, which resulted in his acting-out with drugs and alcohol. This led him to withdraw from life and his close relationships and led to a shutting down of his energy. Mark had also been on a psycho-spiritual journey for the last four years, embracing the work of David Deida, Jiddu Krishnamurti, and Herman Hesse's "Siddhartha." Like most, he was seeking the golden prize of peace and happiness. He also participated in many bio-energetic healing sessions and extensive meditation retreats as a means of finding resolution to his pain. However, he reported feeling continually frustrated and in pain and was hoping a nondual perspective would be helpful.

While acknowledging the benefits of his prior work, I offered the perspective that the experience of *no-self* can be an important transformative agent. As we allow the peeling away of our conditioned identity, the possibility of realizing truth becomes available. "That's what Siddhartha saw and what Krishnamurti always spoke about, isn't it?" Mark asked. I nodded in reply and responded that awakening is already the case right now. Awakening is the realization that there is no separate self apart from existence. The dream is in believing we are strictly our thoughts, that we are bound by our bodily impulses and emotional states. And since Mark was somewhat familiar with the spiritual journey, I pointed out that the natural stateless state of *no-self* is the fundamental condition of who and what we are in the present moment, and that, although there are no guarantees, perhaps seeing the various dimensions of our traumas in the light of *no-self* could be transformative. With this, Mark was open to the invitation.

I had the opportunity to work with him for about three months on a weekly basis, and the following is a brief account of some of our work together. I wanted to highlight some of Mark's breakthrough experiences. The first several sessions dealt with exploring the history of his trauma and pointing out the stateless state of *no-self*. There was a tendency for Mark to become caught in his story. So rather than fixating on it, I fluctuated between acknowledging the importance of his story and his feelings and introducing unconditional awareness. It took some time and repeated encouragement, but Mark was able to relax the grip on his stories and have some "glimpses" of unconditional mindfulness and relax into it. When the opportunity arose, I would point out the awareness prior to his mind and stories of what happened in his past. I would do this by saying, "Notice what sees and experiences this?" or "Notice what is aware of these thoughts and feelings?" This helped sever the magnetic identification he had with the content of his mind and feeling states. He could relax that much more and allow the deeper and more difficult states and happenings surrounding his trauma to emerge.

Our eighth session became transformative for Mark and something I would like to highlight here. He arrived at our session feeling heavy and helpless. He described a deep pain residing within the middle of his chest. While inquiring further, Mark shared that his form of helplessness was in relation to not being able to protect himself during moments of abuse from his father. It appeared that underneath his recollection of the traumatic event was a series of judgements, including, "This shouldn't have happened, I should have been able to protect myself, and why didn't my mother stop it?" Here, I encouraged him to stay with his state of helplessness completely, not to judge it, or try and change it in any way. With continued support, he was able to tolerate his experience, allowing it to open up further. His prior work of dis-identifying by remaining as a witnessing consciousness helped him here. As a result, this seemed to propel Mark into deeper recesses of his being. While hunched over in his chair and with closed eyes, he appeared eclipsed by a form of fear. He was visibly shaking. Within this state, he reported experiencing himself as standing in the middle of a large coliseum, similar to the ancient ones built during the days of the Roman Empire, where he could see thousands of disfigured ghost-like images yelling and cursing inaudible accusations at him – some of which were even re-enacting traumatic events from his life. While recoiling out of fear, his body seemed to tighten up as a means of protecting and defending himself. Mark appeared noticeably terrorized.

To avoid a total collapse of his consciousness or even suffer the debilitating effects of dissociation, I suggested he not participate in the imagery and focus his awareness on the emerging fear and see it as energy instead. Our need to label our feelings often prevent the naturally free-flowing of them, and by de-labeling emotions and seeing them as energy, we allow the dammed-up force to flow naturally. Mark did as I suggested and experienced a radically different relationship with his fear. He noticed the energy of fear move on its own, doing what it needed to do, and this allowed him more space to simply be with the unfolding experience. He was able to tolerate the energy of fear without judgement or the need to run and avoid it. The tension in his body lessened greatly.

With tears rolling down his eyes, and to his amazement, Mark reported seeing himself now as a point of brilliant light in the middle of the coliseum, and that, although the phantom-like figures were still present, there was no fear. I then asked him to merge with that point of light. To be that empty space, here and now. With this, he felt the point of light filling his entire being, leaving him feeling light and expansive. The imagery of his vision suddenly dissolved, and he felt surprisingly peaceful and relaxed.

Every Evening Comes the Moon

As Mark opened his eyes, tears continued to roll down his face as we sat in silence together, appreciating the depth of his experience. Very little was said at this point outside of Mark sharing that his tears were of compassion and love, and he no longer felt identified with his psychological history. We honored this by spending the remainder of our session relaxing in the stillness and silence of the moment. Freedom from the self relaxes one's inner psychological and emotional resistance where the frozen moments of trauma are thawed and healed. We no longer are bound by our traumatic history.

I was quite touched by Mark's experience as it mirrored elements of my own years ago. I also recognize that a lot of Mark's prior therapeutic work and involvement in the spiritual journey helped him in making these breakthroughs, which may not have been the case for people not familiar with the journey of awakening and self-discovery. Mark and I met for several more sessions where he reported the states of peace and relaxation had subsided, and so came the return of his mental chatter, whereby he began to doubt the validity of his previous experience. I helped normalize this by describing it as the mind trying to reassert itself. Many spiritual teachers have warned of this, sharing there is an error in believing awakening is a one-time shot deal. I pointed out to Mark that awakening is a moment-to-moment journey – how awake we are in this moment is what matters, and with that, we both smiled, recognizing this moment is all there is. Eternity abides *here and now*.

In the next section, we'll explore the new moon and how it gives way to the first quarter moon, which represents the very real challenge of living an awakened life. As we abide deeper into our true nature, the task is to live an embodied life where we are an expression of truth and we live the uncompromising truth of our realizations in every aspect of our lives.

Part 4 – The First Quarter Moon: The Challenge of Embodied Awakening in Everyday Life

> *Before enlightenment chop wood, carry water. After enlightenment chop wood, carry water.*
>
> - Zen Proverb

"Baby, my chakras are all blown open and I'm just marveled at the mystery of it all!" "That's beautiful honey, now here's the grocery list, pick this up after work, and don't forget the cat litter needs to be changed as well." There is a nondual saying that if you really want to know how awakened someone is, just ask their partner. We can have blissed out experiences and be opened up to our true nature, but life carries on, bills need to be paid, laundry needs to be done, and marriages need attending to. Just because we have realized the truth does not mean the rest of our lives continue to be free of pain and suffering. Awakening has nothing to do with improving one's life or making it easier. Suffering continues to exist, poverty continues to exist, unpaid bills and job losses continue to exist – the difference now though, is that it is nothing personal. Life continues as it did, although there is now the deepening realization that it's happening to no one. The first quarter moon is used as a way of representing the need for an embodied awakening in all aspects of life. Now that we have had a taste of our true nature, the task is to live life from this realization amongst our friends and family, while at work, and while paying bills and doing the laundry. There is a misconception that having experienced the truth of one's being, means one needs to live a monastic life, shave their head, live in a commune or a cave, and leave their life behind. That may or may not happen but know that it has nothing to do with how awakened you are. The embodied awakening I'm speaking to – and that many others speak of as well – is living a realized life now, in the midst of the life we are currently living. The Sufis speak of "being in the world, but not of it," which is the essence of embodied awakening.

Even though a person may have seen through the belief in the separate self, there still exists an apparent personality that engages the world, there is still an apparent someone who needs to maintain a life. The questions become then: "Has awakening touched my inner and outer life? Am I an expression of truth with the ones I love and while at work? Or am I 'hoarding' awakening and reserving it for special occasions and with certain people? Am I only awake at weekly *Satsangs*, nondual workshops, and conferences and resort back to old-conditioned ways of being with my partner and family when I return home? Can we really live an embodied awakening in every area of our life, from the mundane to the extraordinary?"

I'll explore these questions in the following chapters. Let's start by describing how these scenarios can play out with those closest to us, our family and friends.

Chapter 1: Embracing Aloneness in Relationships: Moving Beyond Family Obligations and Social Contracts

Yes, you who must leave everything that you cannot control
It begins with your family, but soon it comes around
to your soul

- Leonard Cohen

Now that we can begin to trust our own unfolding process and abide further into the truth of who we are, the invitation is to live this realization in relationship with those closest to us. This is no cake walk either. There is no way to predict how this will unfold. It often gets messy as a great deal of our identity is tied up and consolidated by those closest to us, especially our parents. To journey outside the expectations of others is to become a stranger amid the status quo. The beliefs and messages about who we are, how to behave and interact, what to believe, who to like and dislike, what to value, and essentially, how to be in the world, need to be confronted. This means addressing those contracts we have made with our loved ones. These pacts are usually mutually agreed-upon ways of being in the world with other people who are close to us as a means of fitting in, belonging, having a role in life, saving face, and being mirrored in a special way. They give us a sense of self, safety and security, and a place within existence. It can look a little something like this: You play the role of the wise father, and I'll play the part of the obedient son. I won't share my intensity with you for fear of being too much and upsetting you. We're friends for life simply because we share a lengthy history of experiences together. We're the "family comes first" pact in which we stick together no matter what. That's all well and good, from the perspective of self, however, from a perspective of truth, it's all relative.

Awakening does not make such deals. Awakening holds no contracts. Awakening is total freedom to be who and what we are. When we are bound by a social or family pact, we sell ourselves out. When we live from a contract of *how to be*, we give up our freedom and the possibility for others to be themselves. Unfortunately, some people attempt to reconcile this through renouncing their entire family and friends and choosing to live a monastic life. Even though this may happen, which is perfectly fine, it's not what I am talking about here, and it is not a reflection of a more awakened life. Centuries ago, living a monastic life may have been what was called for due to the conditions arising at that particular time, but now, perhaps there isn't such a need. The *dharma wheel* has turned and there is a call to share the truth without having to go anywhere. This means being vulnerable in our connections and challenging the ways we have been living and being with friends and family. We are more apt to invite a deeper and more intimate connection with the ones we love by breaking through the limits of interacting and behaving with one another. There exists a much richer and fuller possibility of bonding when we allow ourselves and others to be who we all are. This is the greatest gift we can give to each other. When we are *awake*, we meet others where they are, we meet them in whatever experience they happen to be in. When *awake*, we see ourselves in them; there is no separation or division. It isn't a mental insight; it is a living experience.

There is Only Connection

Of course, not everyone is so thrilled to hear of our new-found discovery and realizations about living an awakened life. Not everyone we love is happy for us and open to hearing about our experiences. Alan and Nancy, two people I interviewed many years ago, who have been on a lengthy journey of awakening, shared their personal accounts of this. For Nancy, her social network fell apart:

> *Nobody has anything to do with me anymore from my law practice. Nobody, not my clients, and not my colleagues and not my friends from that period because they are not interested in me unless I'm also interested in status and prestige. They're all gone. There are a few that phone occasionally, but there was a lot of social life there that's gone. I don't have the social interaction on the surface anymore, at all. So, I used to have a very active social life with people that I knew a little, what I would call a social acquaintance, where social interests were simply exchanged. Those are gone completely.*[xxiii]

For Alan, his father expressed grave concern about his changes and transformations:

I was in India and I wrote a letter to Papaji (spiritual teacher) telling him I loved him. So, I wrote a letter to my dad saying, 'How come I can tell this old Indian man that I loved him and that I never told you that?' Because I was raised British, I was very reserved. So, I wrote my dad this letter and then I said, 'I just want to tell you that I love you.' Two to three months later, I fly into Vancouver and my brother meets me at the airport and says, 'Dad thinks you're in a cult.' I understand where he was coming from you know, and then in the end he's just him. He's just, he's this. There was a lot of acceptance of whoever was doing what.[xxiv]

Family and friends are all a relative concept, life is based on connection. Where there is a bond, there is real intensity, authenticity, freedom, and love. We become mirrors for each other, accepting one another for who we are – this is what we crave as human beings. To be accepted for who we are, not for what others believe us to be. Interestingly, there is also the pattern of regressing back to an early state of being when in the company of family. The mind is a master of self-survival. In my late 20's, I was in a relationship with a woman for a few years, and we would visit her family a lot, and the moment she stepped into their home, she instantly regressed back into a teenager – she would fall into a *little daddy's girl* role. She appeared to drop into this way of being as a means of keeping harmony and a sense of familiar continuity with everyone. I felt like I did not even know who she was anymore, leaving me feeling a little disorientated during our visits. It was difficult to relate, connect, and express myself because I was dealing with a whole new personality.

The problem is that most of our connections with people are based on these deals we have made with one another and so they are inherently limiting and binding, leaving us feeling strangled in being and unable to fully share our energy with humanity. When we place demands on other people and with ourselves to be and perform in a certain way, we are living a lie. It becomes a contract and a relationship based on an agreement and is not authentic, which leaves us imprisoned within the superficial realm of relating and being. When we make a deal with someone, we can feel ourselves beginning to contract and harden, becoming a solid mass incapable of flow and authentic relating. At some point in time, someone's going to have to break that contract; it's inevitable; there will be the feeling of selling out, and that can only go on for so long. It will be tiring and draining. If we are exclusively identified with a role and a particular way of relating in the world, we are living in the mind and tiptoeing through existence. It represents another dead zone of existing. People are afraid to be themselves for fear of upsetting the order of things and tarnishing the family image. But we must risk it all for the truth because truth does not negotiate. Everything is at stake, even our connections with our beloved friends and family. Fear guides our little pacts we've made as, without them, we start to feel lost and adrift in existence with nothing to anchor ourselves to. But this is all projected fear to keep the mind intact. The more aligned we are with the truth of our being, the more it begins to feel nauseating to live such a lie.

The amount of energy and investment we have in our connections to support and strengthen our personal identity is phenomenal. Even with a powerful awakening experience, we can be stunned to find ourselves pulled right back into a regressive rule and role of belonging. The challenge then is to stay in our own energy and awareness and not get pulled into the dramas of other people's lives or their projections of who we are. Staying in our own energy means not getting pulled into other people's emotional and mental stories. The task is to be authentic in our ties, even if that means challenging the friendship or relationship altogether.

It means we are also open to receiving feedback and allowing it to touch us as a means of embracing a deeply genuine bond with someone. It also means that nothing is for certain, connections come and go, and there is no guarantee found in relationships. Living the scripts of "family is everything" or "I'll never leave you," actually keeps us stuck. It limits freedom. Who can actually know for certain what is going to happen? Letting go of such scripts, deals, and contracts can actually bring people closer together. I found this in my own life. By letting go of certain ways of relating with my own family, I found myself reconnecting with them in a more genuine way. Roles are dropped and people can fall in tune with their essence and be who they are without fear of reprisal. This is one of the most beautiful gifts one can give another, the simple acceptance of being who they are.

As we embrace this new way of relating and being, we need to be aware of how the mind can attempt to abort this process for fear of being totally alone. We have come to fear aloneness and avoid it at all costs because we have believed it to be a negative state. We have been taught to constantly be in a relationship, seeking one another out to feel fulfilled, to feel like a somebody. People have this fear they are going to die alone, and so they scatter about desperately looking for someone to attach themselves to, to give themselves a sense of place and stability. It is all counterintuitive, though. By running around chasing the security and connection of another person, it actually leaves us in a constant state of insecurity, anxiety, and a profound sense of being lost. We have to confront our loneliness and accept it. From aloneness, we have the opportunity to make real contact with people because we are not in a desperate need to be seen, liked, or needed by the other person. Aloneness, at its root, means *all one*. We are one with everything, unified and connected with everything and everyone, and by accepting our fundamental isolation, our *all-oneness*, we are accepting the wisdom of insecurity and the uncompromising resolve to simply be who we are.

As Aloneness, we are a pure presence of Awareness; there is no sense of self that needs to be seen or loved in order to feel like one exists. We exist as a presence of love. Solitude has depth of peace, clarity of being, and an unwavering recognition of who we are. Accepting aloneness is like returning home to being, to who we are, and from here, a thriving connection is possible.

Chapter 2: Embracing Mother Kali: The Destroyer of Codependent Relationships

> *Ma Kali is a nurturing presence of the great Mother dwelling in the cavern of our hearts. She opens up all doors to the heart pouring into it her blood, the blood of Divine light and freeing our soul from the shackles of maya, darkness and ignorance.*
>
> - Shambhavi L. Chopra

Under stress, the parts of our conditioned selves that have yet to be seen through become activated and a dominating force in our life. This is apparent in the family cycle of addiction. The trauma of living with an addicted loved one can give rise to codependency. I have had the opportunity to work with many people, particularly with women on the journey towards wholeness who have fallen into the trap of codependency when living with an addicted loved one. Codependency is a dysfunctional helping relationship where one is caught in patterns of enabling, enmeshment, and trying to control another person's addictive behavior. It is a sense of not feeling whole and complete now. It is needing someone to fill the emptiness and the need. This leads to a lack of unhealthy boundaries and emotional and psychological dysfunction. Codependency arises out of intense fear and terror that our loved one will die because of their addiction, so our desire to help them and express compassion becomes distorted – even pathological because it is based on fear.[xxv]

This was often the case with the women I worked with. In order to feel whole and complete, she needs the other to experience the same. Her experience of wholeness is tied up into the other where the frame of reference is: "If he's not complete, I'm not complete." "If he's in pain, I'm in pain." Wholeness is dictated by the other. She is lost in the duality of self and the other, and she starts doing things she thought she would never do, putting herself at risk and in danger. What were once loving and caring traits have now become overbearing, controlling, and manipulative ones. Anger, fear, and anxiety become her dominant states of being, where she is constantly monitoring and advising her loved one, keeping moment-to-moment tabs on their every move, and questioning who they are associating with. This pattern can continue even after the loved one has embraced a period of long-term recovery. It is a form of constant anxiety and distress. There is no sense of boundaries, and many times, she strongly believes she holds the keys to life and death. The energy of life and death is so pervasive and all-consuming for her that she believes the moment she says *no* to her child's demands, the fear of death becomes a reality.

Codependency is a contraction of the heart. She is so enmeshed in her loved one's life of addiction and suffering that she has lost all sense of her own being and nondual flow. Her expression is one of reaction instead of response. She loses the capacity to feel and express love and compassion in a clear and direct way. Her vision has become clouded, and she is easily pulled back into separation, fear, and turmoil. In its chronic form, the mind seizes on these moments of fear and stress because it gives one a sense of busyness, distraction, and self-importance. It allows her to seek outside of herself and become chronically involved in her loved one's life and never-ending crises and dramas. I have heard many women share how they would not know what to do with themselves if they got off the rollercoaster of codependency. Their identity is so wrapped up in the other. Some secretly revealed they derived a considerable amount of self-identity, worth, and value out of being their loved one's rescuer. It's interesting to see how quickly we give up all of our nondual insights and way of being in the world when faced with severe stress. Over time though, she begins to lose all functioning in her day-to-day life and loses connection with the Essence of who she is. It's as if all of her nondual insights disappeared out the window.

The Limits of Traditional Approaches to Healing Codependency

Traditional approaches to healing codependency can be initially helpful, but they only go so far in light of nondual awakening. Although useful and healing when it comes to setting healthy boundaries, establishing assertive communication, and understanding the cycle of family addiction, traditional approaches continue to reinforce the idea of the self and the other and do not fully address the fear and terror lurking within one's being. The result is there continues to be a pattern of tension in her being, as if she is just holding on, anticipating the next crisis. Humbled, I have even found some of my nondual interventions and invitations falling flat to the point where some of the women I have worked with shared that I just didn't understand or even get it altogether. Fortunately, I have some very strong, awakened women in my life. Some very dear friends, who pointed out I needed to be aware of the trap of hyper-masculinity, which is found in many spiritual traditions and meditative practices that may mirror a depth of surrender and acceptance with all things, and if left unchecked, is interlaced with a disconnected, isolated, and idealistic way of being; an absolutist approach that prioritizes the realization of true nature over that of human existence altogether.[xxvi]

Men tend to gravitate towards a full-tilt guns blazing approach to realizing their true nature, who are often depicted as isolated and alone in their practices and understandings and as adopting a crazy wisdom type approach. Whereas women seem to be more receptive, grounded, and relational where there is very little need to display their awakening and realizations. There is transformative power found in a deeply vulnerable and personal way of being in the world. The lure of transcendence can push aside the very real-world problems we encounter as humans, creating a split in our being whereby we are no longer embodying an awakened life. Women are soulfully fed through relationship, transformed in mutuality, and this needs to be appreciated if any significant transformation is to take place. Transforming a codependent relationship, particularly within the context of family addiction, requires a loving fierceness – and this is where the mother archetype of Kali comes in.

Embracing the Mother Kali Archetype

The mother archetype is an energetic collective pattern of consciousness that extends throughout all cultures and traditions. When we think of the mother archetype, figures throughout history who embody compassion, caring, protective, and sympathetic traits come to mind, such as the images of Mother Mary, Eve, the Motherland, and Mother Theresa. We can see here how these mothering traits would naturally become intensified when faced with the perils of a loved one's addiction. The problem though, due to the crisis and chaos involved in dealing with family addiction, what was once a naturally open, caring, and compassionate set of heartfelt motherly traits, has now become distorted and pathological. What was once compassion has now morphed into compulsive compassion – where out of fear and terror she screams, "If I don't give him money, he'll steal from someone or get shot," or "If I don't let her stay with us she'll freeze to death out on the street." She may have convinced herself that she is doing the right thing by protecting her loved one from the consequences of addiction; however, she is doing nothing but reinforcing the addictive pattern and her own limitations. Enabling and codependency has now become her primary state of being. Love and compassion has turned into fear and control. Anger and resentment lay buried in her consciousness. She has become so invested in her loved one's struggles that she has lost any sense of who she is and is completely at a loss about what to do. The mind has taken over, and she is lost in illusion. She is depleted of vitality and locked in the prison of addiction herself. The mind is overly activated and heavily invested in the outcome of her child's life to the point of putting herself at risk.

This is where I have found the archetypal energy of Mother Kali to be very useful in deepening one's journey of *self-realization* and addressing the patterns of codependency. Mother Kali represents destruction and is often depicted as a black, fierce, and frightening figure dressed in ornaments of death and destruction. But it's important to realize:

Kali is not some mere folk deity, some ancient Goddess, or a strange object for intellectual curiosity or cultural image. She is the Supreme Power of magical, awesome, cataclysmic universe in which we live, of which we are all but brief expressions, and to which we must all bow down in reverence in the end. Kali holds our life and our death within her embrace that is kind to the soul but can be painful to the ego, delaying or restricting the soul's unfoldment. Purification, which implies the destruction of negativity, must precede any creation or transformation. Kali provides that purification but brings about the new creation and transformation as well. Her destructive force is only for the destruction of negativity, limitation and sorrow – an invitation for us to look beyond the boundaries of death, suffering and ego, to an inner reality not touched by these shadows.[xxvii]

Her fierce expression is a purification force. A fierce, loving, and compassionate energy, which embraces life and death, pain and suffering, and is an opening to one's true nature. Her loving fierceness matches the intensity found in codependent relationships and family addiction. The fierceness of Kali is what destroys her own states of fear, doubt, confusion, and states of anxiety and separation, while manifesting a new way of relating and responding to her struggling loved one. The energy of Kali facilitates a nondual way of being, a way of being where one is anchored in Truth and embodies its wisdom in everyday life – the self and other split is seen through where she feels as though she is inside the other – she is totally the other. She may understand she is not really doing anything to help her loved one, yet she seems to respond in an authentic, and what may even be considered helpful way, by others – the difference is that it does not register as such. There is no ownership of it, it was really just a natural spontaneous expression of love; love that is direct, transcendent, and lovingly fierce. She is a presence that can hold the paradox of life and death in the moment and respond naturally with that which is in line with the truth. It is a compassionate presence that is not demanding or self-centered. It is such a loving presence which does not hold the perspective that there is something *wrong with you*, and there is no one saying, "I am full of love and compassion." There is just an organic expression of love and compassion in the moment. She is nothing but an expression of love. Love is who she is and it is in the absence of who she is that the opportunity to heal and transform can take place.

Rita's Journey

Rita had been working with the energy of Kali for a couple of years and was learning to embody the loving tenderness of the heart and ferocity of Kali in many areas of her life. She was becoming much more spontaneous, loving, and direct with people. She was quite the whirlwind of energy and in the nondual flow when she participated in one-to-one sessions and group work with me. At one moment, she could radiate a vast loving heart, interconnected with all things, a compassionate presence, and in the next, it seemed like she could destroy anything in her way with just a look. Then, it was when her 22-year-old son, Eric, moved back into her home that Rita was put to the test. Eric struggled with a chronic addiction problem for many years, and because he lived in another province at the time, Rita was better able to manage him from a distance. However, the moment she allowed him to move into her home, she fell into constant states of crisis and turmoil. Her flowing *beingness* was replaced by a presence of perpetual tension and confusion. She resorted to a codependent way of being with him, trying desperately to get him to quit at the expense of her own well-being. Eric was involved in selling drugs, and for the last several months, Rita shielded him from all the consequences associated with his lifestyle, from making excuses for him at work, giving him money, and suffering verbal and emotional abuse. And things intensified quickly when she found out Eric was hiding drugs somewhere on her property.

Rita met with me for an emergency one-to-one session appearing energetically depleted and saddened. She was living a day-to-day crisis, and she knew she was heading for disaster. She was desperately trying to control something that was totally out of her control. She knew she could be held liable for knowingly remaining silent about her son's involvement in criminal activity. She was at a breaking point, and I felt like the moment was ripe to ask, "Can you see how everything you have done up to now has been completely hopeless? All this Mother Theresa loving kindness stuff really hasn't helped you, has it?" "I know, I know," she cried. "What happened to all the Kali energy? Wouldn't this be the time to really embody her?" I shared. "I'm afraid he's going to get killed or be on the street," she cried again. Her mind was spinning with worst case scenarios. There was a lot of ego activity taking place, so we spent some time slowing things down and staying present in the moment instead of identifying with all her stories. "Notice how the mind is racing around with all these stories that haven't happened. I can appreciate the very real feeling of fear, but how about not adding to it with all these stories. Let's see if we can relax the attention on the mind at this moment," I said. Rita seemed to hone in on this, and together we sat in silence for a few minutes so she could dis-identify from all of her inner chatter.

She breathed out a sigh of relief and nodded slowly, "Okay, yeah, this is helping, I'm here." Rita seemed to relax and allow a quality of spaciousness into her experience. "And the fear?" I asked. "It's still here, it's intense but I'm staying with it without my usual stories." "Good, very good," I replied. "You've done everything you can to help your son, but nothing has worked; you've done things you would normally never have done, and the fear of him dying keeps you on the rollercoaster of codependency. Now maybe what is needed is that loving fierceness of Kali I've come to see you embrace over the years. Now, this might be hard to hear at first, but what would it be like to simply allow your son to play out whatever is destined for him to play out, to totally let go, and see that you are not in control of any of this?" I wasn't suggesting that Rita completely cut herself off from Eric but for her to connect with the underlying spaciousness she was experiencing and power within. "There's a part of myself that is so scared to lose him. I'm so scared he'll die," she replied. The fear of losing him was so strong, and her body was beginning to tremble. "Stay as the spaciousness, and be with your experiences with no judgement," I said to her. I didn't want to console her with any hope-based strategies that would reinforce and resurrect the patterns of codependency.

She seemed a little more at ease sitting with her fear, so I also invited her to sit in the energy of life and death right now without trying to control it. I invited her to see how we are each just temporary beings of light destined to play out our karmic patterns in whatever form. I suggested that perhaps this life of hers was meant for her to learn the depth of letting go and surrendering to existence. She did not seem to react to this and reported being able to be with this realization more deeply. She reported feeling more relaxed and not grasping at her mind and the needing to control as much. She saw that her previous attempts at trying to help her son was in fact perpetuating the cycle of addiction. "By seeing him as being a problem, I become the problem," she stated. Tears were rolling down her cheeks, and she seemed much more relaxed. She did not appear tense, and I could tell something had suddenly shifted for her. She described an image in her mind's eye of how her son and the rest of her family, for that matter, were all just dancing sparks of light flickering spontaneously. It was such a beautiful image that I asked her to stay with it for a while and to see what happened next. After a few minutes, she reported that they were all of a sudden being blown out and becoming puffs of smoke. I felt it was very important for her to stay with this experience and encouraged her not to judge it since what was being revealed to her was very significant. I invited her to stay with it and to notice the interconnecting energy of it all, the black empty space of awareness.

I wanted to see if we could bring this realization deeper into her relationship with Eric, so from here, I asked Rita, "What would you say from this place, from this place of loving ferocity where you are no longer begging and making deals or pandering to his every need?" Immediately, she welled up with tears, "God this is so hard, I don't know, I don't know what I would say." Rita was starting to shut down into fear and immobility. Spaciousness was given over to fear and separation. I didn't want her to lose the open expansive state she had felt earlier, so I invited her to externalize the situation. I invited her to role-play with me where I would be Eric, and she could say whatever it was she needed to say to him. She made eye contact with me and smiled slightly, which seemed to bring her out of her shut down mode. "Rita," I said. "I invite you to take a few moments and see me as Eric, and say whatever it is you need to say to him, but to come from that loving fierceness place of no-deal making." Rita stared at me from across the room, and I could sense a great deal of anger and rage building up in her, and she let me have it. "You're fucking killing yourself!! What the hell is wrong with you? I didn't raise you like this!" She screamed. Rita went on for several minutes, sharing her energy directly with me, expressing all of her pent-up anger and rage. "How do you feel now? What are you noticing?" I asked. "There's lots of energy running through me, but I notice that I'm clearer, like I have more awareness or something." "Can you see that your motivation to save him, help him, and solve his problems is actually reinforcing things and throwing you into identification and limitation; into cycles of fear and reactivity?" I asked. She nodded in agreement, "Yeah, fear, fear has been ruling my whole world lately." "Remember," I shared, "Fear is self-centered; love isn't. Love is free from the notion of self and other, and it is from love that we respond to life in a free, direct, and spontaneous way. Kali doesn't make any deals, she is fierce and direct, but she also has a vast loving heart, and it is love that transcends fear and limitation." After now having moved through some of her fear, anger, and rage, I invited Rita to visualize the image of Kali in her mind's eye and to bring her awareness into her heart and notice what happened next. After several moments she shared, "Jesus, I feel so much love, … I love him so much. I see him and all of his confusion, pain, and struggles and the possibility that he might die if he doesn't do something for himself." After a few moments, I asked, "And what's happening for you now?" "It's strange," she said. "There's so much sadness here, but I'm okay with it." I let this statement hang for a while as we sat in silence together for the remainder of our session.

We met for a few more sessions over the next several weeks when she was able to integrate and clarify her experiences, realizations, and understandings. It was important they become a living reality for her. Eventually, Rita did make the decision to have Eric removed from her home. Although she reported it as being one of the most difficult decisions in her life, she recalled our work together and drew upon the powerful archetypal energy of Kali by allowing things to play themselves out without the need for a particular outcome. She did not give into the mind, and she was able to surrender to the realization that she had no control over Eric's life, which paradoxically freed her up to respond more effectively. Embodying the energy of Kali allowed Rita to burn through her codependent patterns and embrace a deeper reality of nondual being in her everyday life.

Chapter 3: Wide Awake Around the Water Cooler: Taking Down the Petty Tyrant at Work

My benefactor used to say that a warrior who stumbles on a petty tyrant is a lucky one.

- Carlos Castaneda

Nondual awakening calls for us to be a blown-wide open presence of being; a vast openness in the presence of challenging life circumstance. It's a call for "warriorship" – not the call to arms type of warrior, but of an open-hearted fierceness, where existence is met as it is no matter what presents itself. All too often, people on the awakening journey adopt an overly passive approach to life of avoiding challenging encounters with others, not being open to receiving constructive feedback, and dismissing others as being "too aggressive" if they portray any type of wild nondual intensity. I've seen this take place at nondual conferences and within therapeutic groups, where people who would share their intense no deal making wild energy would just get dismissed and labeled as "crazy wisdom" or even pathologized as not having fully surrendered. Sometimes, they would be removed from a group or presentation altogether or be ignored and kept at a distance. It's as if passivity has become the hallmark of awakening in some spiritual circles. But life beckons for intensity; life calls for fierceness in the face of difficulties. Awakening asks for us to share our nondual intensity, which can arise as a beautiful "sublimeness" or white-hot fierceness. Awakening can be seen in a soft and gentle gesture of appreciation and compassion or in the form of a fiery passion of direct communication. Life has a way of shaking us up – of testing us in a fundamental way. The vast majority of humanity lives in division, separation, and conditioning. Society sells us the quest for self-identity, self-improvement, and individuation. Society sells us fear and desire and the need to consume. To step out of that is to step out of the herd. To step out of the herd is to embrace an uncompromised fierceness of living one's truth; it is to lose our self-importance, and frankly, people don't like that, so we get tested in a variety of ways to see just how deep our awakening really goes. And a petty tyrant is just one advisory who can test us at a deep level.

Spiritual teacher, Carlos Castaneda, describes a petty tyrant as someone who shows up in your life to nag you, aggravate you, frustrate, and annoy you to no end to push you beyond the brink. They are typically people in positions of power who interrupt, endlessly annoy, challenge, and frustrate one to death. But here's the thing, to find a petty tyrant in our life is to find someone who will help us drop our own sense of uniqueness and specialness in the world. Instead of running from a petty tyrant, we are invited to change our perceptions and see them as an opportunity for growth and transformation. The insignificant oppressor can help reveal what it is we are still hanging on to, what we are defending against, what our limitations are, and what has been a mere nondual belief rather than a living truth. They can help us transform our own sense of self-importance.

They can serve as a mirror, reflecting back to us what we have kept hidden within ourselves, what we haven't worked through, and what we haven't yet let go of. There is the possibility to co-exist with a petty tyrant, but there are times when this is not the case.[xxviii]

You see, we can be coasting along in nondual bliss, and then all of a sudden, bump up against one of these tyrants who challenge us endlessly. Frustrated and annoyed, we fall back into states of division and separation, where we become reactionary and defend ourselves vigorously. Under such stress, we fall back into our own sense of self-importance, as if a curtain of consciousness closes, and we lose access to our own awakened insights and flowing *beingness*. Here, we fall into the perpetual states of anger, frustration, and loss of control and clarity.

This doesn't have to be our destiny when confronted with a petty tyrant, though, as we can embrace the possibility of transformation in such an encounter. When we embrace an energetic fierceness, we express it in the spirit of play, meaning we see that life is a dance of contradictions, so we can match a petty tyrant without taking it so personally. We can play, joust, and "bob and weave" like a boxer; we can dance with a nasty bully before taking them down, knowing full well it is all a game. A risky, intense, and dangerous game, but a game, nonetheless. Who could possibly be defeated when having been extinguished of our own self-importance? I'm reminded of the Taoist verse in the Tao Te Ching by Lao Tzu, "When two great forces oppose each other, the victory will go to the one that knows how to yield."[xxix]

This is the perspective to come from when confronted with such an advisory

Taking Down a Petty Tyrant at Work

I bumped into my own petty tyrant at work, and it seems that with most people I have spoken to and worked with, the workplace is the best place to find a nasty bully because it is where we spend most of our time and life energy. I was a supervisor at a government run counselling centre when I ran into her; I will call her Karen. Although Karen was not my primary boss, I did have to meet with her on a regular basis and account for my clinical work. She was upper management, and she had regular contact with me. She was a master of delegation and condescension and strategically blocked career moves. Not only that, but she made life very difficult for me; she presented as the typical sort; smug and condescending in tone and regularly needled me about my counselling style and interventions. Anything outside the run-of-the-mill evidenced-based practice style of solution-focused therapy was deemed inappropriate, and she cautioned me that engaging in other forms of counselling work would become part of my performance review. For years, I had free reign to facilitate transpersonal and nondual interventions in my work with clients, but all of a sudden, she wanted to put an end to it despite the positive client and counselor feedback about my approach. It felt like she had it out for me. She would give me endless make-work projects that would take me away from my regular work-related duties as a supervisor, question my commitment to the agency, and when I refused to work longer hours, she reported me to the Executive Director, stating I was not on the after-hours on-call list even though it was optional. I did my best to simply avoid her and did my nod and smile routine, but that wouldn't cut it. Over time, I was feeling energetically drained and becoming increasingly angry inside. I learned that some of my friends in various parts of the agency had taken an extended sick leave or outright quit due to her aggressive tactics and micromanagement style. Something was about to give.

I reached my limit the day she pulled me into a meeting with the Executive Director about my handling of a client who had unfortunately stopped taking her medication and was mentally decompensating. So much so that she ended up physically attacking staff and clients, and had planned to harm herself. It was serious enough that for her own safety, I immediately had her involuntarily placed in a psychiatric facility, and because of her violent attacks, it was mandatory that police arrive to help escort her to the facility. Karen questioned me as to why I had not contacted her before making my decisions. I replied that this was standard practice and that, as a seasoned supervisor, I could make these decisions and had informed the manager I reported to. She was not satisfied with this and shared she felt like I was going behind her back. I was confused and frustrated, attempting to share the reasoning behind my decision, but she refused to hear it.

At this point, I had had enough. A counselling position had opened up internally, and I decided to apply for it. It would be a huge pay cut, and it was a couple of steps down from my role as a supervisor, but I was a shoe in for the job, or so I thought. As I arrived for the interview, Karen was on the interview panel. I was shocked! Although I felt I had aced the interview, she told me I was not the successful candidate, and they decided to hire a new person outside the agency with minimal experience.

I went home that night shocked and in disbelief. I had no idea it would be more difficult to descend the corporate ladder than to climb it. My wife suggested I either take an extended sick leave, file a grievance, or quit altogether. I could feel my awareness contracting and becoming crystallized. I was pissed and was personalizing everything. I could have run with this, and I would have been supported by my friends and work colleagues, but something did not feel right about this approach. I appreciated my wife's heartfelt suggestions, but I took a few days to reflect and meditate on my situation. It was early one evening when I remembered Carlos Castaneda's words on how to deal with a petty tyrant:

Brian Theriault

> *The mistake average men make in confronting petty tyrants is not to have a strategy to fall back on; the fatal flaw is that average men take themselves too seriously; their actions and feelings, as well as those of the petty tyrants, are all-important. Warriors, on the other hand, not only have a well-thought-out strategy, but are free from self-importance. What restrains their self-importance is that they have understood that reality is an interpretation we make.*[xxx]

It became clear to me that I had met a petty tyrant. I saw my reactivity, confusion, and anger hardening, which was causing me suffering. I was contracting upon myself, becoming small, foggy, and exhausted. I was taking it way too seriously. Here, my awareness began to expand, my personality loosened, and I felt like I had an entirely different view on the whole thing. My perception had changed. I started to see her as a meditation, an opportunity to transform and grow. Carlos Castaneda outlines the practice of control, discipline, forbearance, and timing to be used in taking down a petty tyrant. Control and discipline refer to a relaxation of the frantic mind, of jumping to conclusions, and making disastrous unconscious decisions. It's also about not getting lost in the stories we tell ourselves about what is happening or readily agreeing with what others share with us. We need to be careful about what we take on and with whom we listen to and agree with, as it will determine our perceptions and actions. Forbearance is the ability to be in a state of patience, ease, and calm but acutely aware and alert at the same time. Awareness is vast and spacious. Here, we have a degree of clarity and precision in our response. Often, we are more of a witness collecting information about our petty tyrant, observing their personality traits and behavior. In essence, we are observing how the mind operates. And timing is the moment of opening up and taking down the petty tyrant. It is a calculated move in which the bully is exposed and collapses under pressure. It is a moment where their sense of power, control, and self-image crumbles.[xxxi]

Earnestly, I reviewed the last three years of my interactions with Karen, particularly over the last eight months, and discovered some valuable information. I knew she was an anxious, insecure person, and she needed constant validation and mirroring from her superiors, particularly from the Executive Director. For the next ten months, I engaged in a form of active meditation where I applied some of the principles of dealing with a petty tyrant. Since she took herself so seriously, I decided to create situations that would place her in a questionable light in front of her boss. I had to do this in a not-so-obvious way, though. I had to set it up so it would not look like I was out to get her. I had to be subtle and let the situation take over while leaving me out of it. Furthermore, as she was responsible for client and community relations, I began to redirect all client complaints and allied professional concerns about the agency to the Executive Director, who then spoke with her about them. As more and more complaints were received, she was becoming increasingly frustrated with herself. As she pulled me into random meetings to question my decisions or give me more make-work type projects as a means of punishing me, I always made sure I followed up with an email summary of our discussions as a means of keeping record and asking her to advise me on how to juggle my schedule. Essentially, I gave her all control, which appeared to overwhelm her. She was starting to drop the ball on projects and decision-making strategies.

Similarly, since she always wanted to be informed of decision-making processes, I started to allow crises to happen in the work place. I stopped fixing everything when they manifested; from client and staff complaints, union issues, policy discrepancies, to lack of internal resources, and turned it all over to her. I would email her with an account of the crisis and ending it with "please advise." I made a large portion of my workload her problem. She would then frequently contact me on my work cell phone after work hours regarding work-related questions and requests. Normally, I would have responded in the past, but I used it as another opportunity. Instead of simply answering the phone and responding to her concerns, I started to record it as overtime pay. A fifteen minute phone call ended up being three hours of overtime pay as per the union agreement. I submitted a number of forms totaling a substantial amount of overtime pay, which eventually reached the ears of her superior. This didn't go over well for her, as budget concerns were always a top priority for the agency.

As the months unfolded, I noticed how much more relaxed and at ease I felt about it, how I felt about my approach and my responses to her. Her verbal jabs and constant needling didn't stick to me as much anymore. Interestingly, I noticed that I was not as angry with her as I used to be. I felt like a hollow bamboo where existence could just pass through me. I was awake, wide awake, and stayed the course. I felt vigilant, calm, and open. I felt so incredibly alive and aware, and the times when I became frustrated, it did not last as long. I did not get as caught up in my own complaints. I learned to trust my process and the path laid out for me. And then, all of a sudden, I stopped receiving any communication from her. I learned through the agency grape vine that she had taken a sick leave. Soon after, she had resigned. I am not suggesting that my change in tact with Karen ultimately led her to take a sick leave and resign – perhaps there were other life issues she was contending with, but the realization I found in this experience is that it is a workable situation. Not only did I notice a drop in my own self-importance, but subsequently, I experienced a deeper sense of compassion, curiosity, and wonder. I did not have to quit my job or demote myself to another role. I found an awakened capacity to meet the challenge in front of me. Karen showed me I could access qualities within me that stretched beyond the confines of a limited self. I felt I could use our interaction as another way of waking up to who and what I truly am.

A warrior is one that is awake and available in any situation. One who is awake and unafraid, full of love and potential, open and free. To be awake is to be the full deck of human consciousness and respond to the moment as needed, from the gentleness and playful giggles of a child to that of embracing the lion's roar.

Chapter 4: Pseudo Digital Enlightenment: The Problem of Facebook Questing and WiFi Awakeness

---

Do you find yourself telling others about your great experience of enlightenment? Sad news is, this is little less than bragging, and as such, it has the prerequisite of an inflated ego. Yes, bragging, social media culture, and most aspects of contemporary life work very well in the favor of our egos.

- Attila Orosz

Got a terrible case of the enlightenment blues? Are you feeling unappreciated for your spiritual brilliance and heartfelt love for the world? Want to set yourself up as the new up-and-coming nondual teacher? Not a problem, set up a Facebook account and send five thousand "friend requests" to whomever, post a clever nondual insight, and boom! Instant *Sangha*. You are now an internet guru, virtually awake, and digitally plugged in. You have free reign to digitally check in and out of your newly created virtual world, posting transcendent pictures of yourself and showing the world how Awake you are. And, as your digital universe expands, you can take it a step further and offer online enlightenment workshops and coaching sessions. Many people are setting up what is characterized as a digital ashram. And, if you ever get pissed off at someone for challenging your most recent nondual post or awakened brilliance, no worries, just "unfriend" them into digital oblivion.

Social media has become an important platform to share the realizations of nondual awakening, however, there's also a shadow side to it. The shadow side of awakening has gone viral on Facebook and other social media platforms. Some people find it too difficult to embody their nondual realizations in day-to-day life, so they resort to projecting an alternate awakened persona – what I call "wifi awakeness." Of course, there is tremendous value in social media as a means of communicating and sharing from a place of embodied awakening, but the problem exists when it is used as a means of escaping the challenges of day-to-day embodied living and posting a persona of being spiritually awake, which does not reflect one's true life. It happens a lot, and the motivation behind it appears to stem from the need to be seen and admired.

Awakening has made its way into the digital playground, where people can hide behind an awakened persona. When we don't have genuine contact with anyone or hold any real meaningful relationships, it is easy to act as an "online guru" and project an image of awakened living. Likewise, it's also easy to be a nondual keyboard warrior, a rogue spiritual "quester" if you will, who likes to stir things up and try to "stump" the online guru and community altogether. In this case, what's occurring online is nothing more than a barrage of projections masquerading as truth. There's no real accountability for one's words and actions, often lacking resonance with what is being pointed to in the journey of self-realization.

It reminds me of the movie *Tron* where people are "downloaded" into a virtual video game; a digital world where they are battling it out with each other, defending their world views, showcasing their wisdom, and forming relationships, all the while the real world continues on as it is.

We can be pulled into believing that something of significance is happening online. This new digital playground can act as a perfect opportunity for the mind to run rampant and for our shadow issues to take full bloom. Recently, there have been a number of spiritual teachers being outed online for questionable behavior and lambasted for their actions. One moment a teacher can present themselves as a loving and awakened being, and then suddenly, someone has dug up their criminal record and posted it online or copy and pasted a previous post of theirs, from a past discussion, that contradicts their current post and shares it for all to see, as a means of exposing them and shutting them down. A person can spend a great deal of time engaging in these "Facebook wars" and lose the passion for embodied awakening and authentic connection.

There appears to be a trend where social media is being used to bypass personal issues when presenting oneself as an awakened being, which is often a far cry from the truth of what's happening in their personal lives. We can fall into the trap of wanting to be seen as unique and an awakened online energy phenomenon. The act of chasing "likes" and amassing as many followers as possible can lead us further away from the truth. The possibility of waking up is missed each time we believe exclusively in the mind to define us or for others to accept and appreciate us. We have to become completely honest with ourselves and ask the question, "Am I living my truth, or am I just escaping pain?" We have to take responsibility, we need to get real with ourselves and investigate and uncover our true motivations. Truth doesn't hide when we begin to honestly look inside ourselves. When we get honest with ourselves at a guttural level, we can begin to feel into the lies and deceits we have been telling ourselves.

If we are indeed lying to ourselves, then our casual viewing and online participation can be seen as a dry, dead way of being in the world, like entombing ourselves in a digital dream land. It ends up being another way in which the mind co-opts awakening by leaving one in a perpetual digital dream state. The situation reminds me of the biblical story of Lazarus. The story goes that when Lazarus died, everyone was upset as he was a beloved member of his community. His body was entombed in a cave rotting and stinking for days, and when Jesus learned of his death, he eased everyone's grief and pain by calling him back to life. Jesus approached the tomb in which Lazarus was kept and yelled, "Lazarus, come out!" Lazarus heard Jesus's words, woke up, and walked out of his tomb to the shock and astonishment of his family and friends. Lazarus exited the cave and joined the awakened and living with clear eyes. Lazarus heard the words of truth and woke up out of his own fixated mind, the cave of self-limitation, and came to realize the truth of his own being.[xxxii] The story of Lazarus is the story of the human condition. When we live in the mind, we are eternally asleep and divorced from truth, but when we hear and apperceive the truth of existence, we log off of the mind and rest in our natural stateless state of being. Today, many of us are entombed in a digital cave, living a fake life, and are asleep to whom we truly are.

Rich's Journey

My friend Rich appeared lost in his own online spiritual wonderland. He called me in a panic wanting to meet for a coffee to talk. His girlfriend had just left him, and he was obviously devastated. She accused him of being emotionally unavailable and distant over the last year and a half. She had enough of him hiding himself up in his office and spending hours online with his "Dharma community," accusing him of pretending to be someone he wasn't. Over the last year, since going online with social media, Rich would spend most of his evenings after work on it, engaging in intense discussions about Buddhism and awakening, where he received a flood of positive mirroring for his intellect and perceived vulnerability. He totally enjoyed it and felt alive and energized by the feedback. The problem, though, was that very little of this translated into the real world with his partner and within his day-to-day life. There was a significant incongruence between his early morning nondual social media status posts and evening dinner conversations with his partner.

Rich portrayed himself as open and vulnerable online, easily connecting with others while sharing his insights and wisdom as if they were a living reality. In true reality, though, his life was falling apart. He was becoming isolated and even emotionally stunted. When he was away from his computer, he was left with himself and the pain of living a split life, an incongruent life. And with no ability to receive rapid positive mirroring from his social media community, he struggled. Rich's insights and realizations of his true nature were not being integrated into his everyday life. His relationship life was becoming a mess. The love and intensity he shared with his girlfriend were drying up fast. It was strange to see my friend, who was learning to embody awakening in many aspects of his life, be swept away in the digital jungle.

One evening, I called him out on it. "Rich, wake up, Donna just left you. You spend more time on the computer trying to set yourself up instead of connecting with those that really love and care about you. You're trying too hard to be someone you're not; you're living in a virtual mind, with virtual friends, and virtual experiences. It's like you're setting yourself up as the next big online guru." "What do you mean?" He replied. "Look at your posts and your pictures, you're claiming to flow along and that you're at one with everything, sharing your wisdom and advice, yet your life is falling apart. I mean, do you even know any of your online friends?" I asked. "Well, I know you," he laughed. "Rich, Donna just gave you some intense feedback about what she sees is going on with the two of you, and you're just blowing it off. What's going on? Where's your vulnerability?" I asked further. He described how he was forming communities and talking about intense transformational work, which is true, but I kept pointing out to him the disconnect I saw with those he is close with, including myself.

It became evident that Rich wanted to be seen as an awakened being. The allure of being perceived as awakened became so intense, he lost connection with the truth of himself and embodied living. There appears to be a level of comfort and safety while online; a person can hide behind the keyboard and project whatever they want to. In Rich's case, there was a struggle in being open and vulnerable in his relationships, mixed with the desire to appear extraordinary. The desire to stand out prevented him from being open in the moment. Osho once warned of this:

Every mind is seeking some extraordinariness. That is what the ego is: always trying to be somebody in particular, always afraid of being nobody, always afraid of emptiness, always trying to fill the inner void by anything and everything. Every human being is seeking extraordinariness – and that creates misery.[xxxiii]

Ordinariness is awakening itself. To be ordinary is to be relaxed into the moment, vulnerable, and free from tensions, desires, and fears; free from the need to be somebody and to be identified in any way. There is no begging for recognition of any kind, so we are not bound by how others perceive us, and as such, we are much more free and willing to share ourselves with the world, whether online or in everyday life. We are not begging to be liked, nor are we reluctant to share our passion with people. There is no need to project an image; we are just a vast presence of being. I wondered if Rich would take the risk and learn to be more vulnerable and ordinary in all aspects of his life, and stop living a split life online and relax into the moment. I pointed this all out to him, but I could tell he was not seeing it, and he carried on his way. Over the next few months, I learned that Rich's relationship did end, and his online presence continued to grow. His experience taught me how easy it is to bypass the rawness of reality if we're not alert enough. Social media allows another fertile opportunity for the mind to project and create an identity and a world that is not real; a world that serves as an escape from life and from the difficult process of embodying our awakened insights in our everyday lives. With instant gratification, mirroring, and access to the global community, we can see how alluring it can be to recreate an online identity; an ideal self-image that doesn't match the living reality of who we are. It's just another illusion of the mind, and one we have to be aware of as we open up to the richness of being.

Chapter 5: Like a Glacial Mountain, Unmoved

Do you not see him,
The really wise man, always at ease, unmoved?
He does not get rid of illusion, nor does
he seek for the (so-called) truth.
Ignorance is intrinsically the Buddha nature,
Our illusory unreal body is the cosmic body.

- Ikkyu

As I sit here and write in the beauty of Nelson, British Columbia, I can't help but pause and look outside my window at the magnificent transcendent beauty of the glacial mountains. They are simply magnificent. The sun beats down on the mountains, with its brilliancy reflected on the snow-covered peaks, while clouds cast massive shadows that stretch out across the deep valleys. The weather can change at any moment. Now I see large dark clouds moving in from the east, and I suspect it won't be long before there is some freezing rain and snow in the forecast. I imagine the rain and snow beating down on the glacial peaks and flowing down into the deep valleys and lake below. The mountain can withstand any weather pattern. It remains completely immobile. Totally anchored to the Earth. As most people take shelter from the rain, the mountains remain untouched, unmoved, and alive as ever. No matter what the weather brings, the mountains remain vast and open to receive.

These gorgeous peaks and the unpredictable weather mirror that of an awakened life. As we learn to stand as awareness deeply anchored in our being, we drop out of the conditioning of the mind. Like the glacial peaks, as awareness, we merely witness the storm of the mind coming and going and remain unidentified and uninvolved with what presents itself. We are an openness to life and can weather any condition. When unidentified from a particular outcome, we can fully respond to life. We are no longer hooked into the problems life brings us. We no longer react and bulldoze our way through life but respond in a clear and open way. Likewise, we live our truth as it has been revealed to us. As awareness, we can ride the peaks and valleys of consciousness, weathering the pleasures and horrors that life brings us.

The clarity of who we are becomes much more apparent, and when we are anchored in truth, we see that who we are cannot suffer. Truth does not suffer or experience any pain whatsoever. Who we fundamentally are cannot be added to or taken away; we are so vast and empty that there are simply no limits. We are a limitless presence embodied in human form. Who we are will always remain, whether there is a body or not. This is why the fear of death only exists in the mind, which is a contraction built upon illusion. The truth of who we are has been here before our birth and will remain ever-present even after our death. The invitation has always been to realize and claim our essential birthright as eternal beings here and now, and to live life in a celebratory way.

Every Evening Comes the Moon

The truth of our being reveals the absence of a centre, someone in control or that needs to be protected. We begin to see we no longer need to defend against life and that there is no need to escape it. Our tensions have been replaced by an overwhelming trust in existence. There is no gap, and there is no wound. Here, we move further away from the tendency to cycle through the distortions and resentments which create the self. The closer we move to the depths of our being, the more we move to a deeper acceptance of what is. Unmoved, there is the absence of needing to prove ourselves to others or trying to stand out as someone special. We learn to abide as nothing and yet are available for everything. Although others may unconsciously project their unresolved karmic conditioning unto us, we remain aware and ready to receive and respond.

Another one of my favourite Zen stories captures this insight brilliantly. It serves as another invitation to embody the realization of being an unmoved mountain. Zen master Hakuin was praised by his village for living the Zen life. However, one day a young girl suddenly became pregnant, and her parents were furious with her. They demanded to know who the father was. It took her some time to confess, but finally, she named Hakuin as being the father. The parents were so angry and confronted Hakuin at his home, yelling and berating him for taking advantage of a young girl. Hakuin simply listened and replied, "Is that so?" When the child was born, the parents brought it to Hakuin to care for. The parents demanded he take care of the child since it was his responsibility. "Is that so?" Hakuin calmly replied and accepted the child as his own. He was seen as a pervert and an outcast, and was shunned by the entire community. About a year later, the mother of the child was haunted by guilt. She eventually told her parents the truth – that the real father of the child was a young man who worked in the fish market. The mother and father of the girl quickly went to Hakuin to ask for his forgiveness, apologize at length, and take the child back. As Hakuin returned the child, he said yet again, "Is that so?"xxxiv

Steve's Journey

Hakuin was an unwavering presence. His story offers us the potential to live an unwavering life, pushed and pulled by the conditions of living. My good friend and colleague, Steve, found himself in a situation where he was invited to stand as a mountain of presence or crumble like an avalanche of reactivity. He was a skilled therapist in a not-for-profit healthcare centre and performed brilliantly. He was a spiritual "quester" himself and would blend Buddhist and Taoist principles whenever he could in his work supervising staff and counselling clients. He was well-liked by staff, as he was seen as a creative, attuned, and skilled therapist; he was even being groomed for upper management. Steve was a shining star at his work place. I have come to appreciate and value my connection with him. Over the years, we have developed a strong working relationship and friendship, which has allowed us to feel comfortable in confiding with one another about our struggles at work and in our own journeys of awakening.

One day, though, I received an emergency phone call from him, sharing he had been accused by Human Resources of "fudging" his expense claims in excess of over four thousand dollars. They said there were a number of "missing receipts" for his out-of-town work-related activities. He was clearly in a panic and kept repeating that all of his expenses were accurate and work-related. I told Steve this was more than likely a finance department error, and that it would be corrected soon. My comments provided minimal relief. His self-image of being the "Golden Boy" at work was cracking under pressure. It would eventually take several weeks for the situation to be resolved. Steve was being accused of lying and knowingly omitting receipts and pocketing the money. When we met for dinner one night after work, he was shaking and trembling and clearly upset. He thought he was going to get fired and felt like everyone was turning on him. Those colleagues who were his perceived friends and "allies" started to distance themselves from him because, naturally, they were also desiring ascension through the corporate ladder, so they did not want to be seen associating with him. He consulted with his union representative, who told him, "All we can ensure is a fair and equitable process." He was informed that "Unless you produce those receipts, there is little we can do." The provincial government took this issue seriously, as there was a crackdown on provincially funded agencies who were caught overspending or double-dipping in any way. He was able to secure copies through his Visa account, but there were still a number of dollars unaccounted for.

I felt for Steve, and I could feel the hugeness of his situation. I could also see how he was adding to his pain. He was weaving many elaborate worst-case scenario stories, which were causing him to be worked up into a frenzy to the point where he even considered taking a stress leave. I pointed this out to him and invited him to slow down his reactivity and stay centered in his being. I shared with him that the more he aggressively defended himself in front of his superiors outside the regularly scheduled meetings meant to address this concern, the more he risked casting doubt. "If you have done nothing wrong, then you have nothing to defend. Stay centered in your being and respond to the situation from there." I said. I could tell this was difficult for him as he had propped up a good image of himself as being the sensitive, skilled, and somewhat rebellious supervisor, which was now all gone. I told him, "If you get hooked into what they are saying about you, if you grab onto it, you will work yourself up into a frenzy. The investigation is continuing, and you will have the opportunity to speak and share your perspective, but try not to let their judgements stick to you outside of the meetings." Life works in this way, one day we are an all-star supervisor, and the next day we are labeled a thief.

We met several more times after that to check in and debrief. I invited Steve to be in this place of "not being liked," and to try and not react to it. I encouraged him to settle into this experience of being seen as a thief and a cheat but not to judge it and remain a witnessing presence. He understood what I was pointing to, although he also started to see how much he prided himself on being seen in a positive light by others. I could see the struggle to relax on his face, as he considered himself a Buddhist, so I asked, "What would Buddha do?" He smiled and appeared to settle more into his being. He appeared to slow down a little, which allowed him the space to be with his experience. Steve nodded in reply as we sat in this recognition together. He saw how he abandoned the truth for personal reactivity and a self-image. He observed how he was lost in his mind. Of course, this wasn't to deny the experiences he was having, as he would need to deal with it, but it served as an invitation to expand beyond the reactive and grasping mind into a much more spacious presence. To respond as presence is freedom from the mind, desired outcomes, and habitual grasping, but it is also a response from clarity, love, power, insight, and directness. It was important to respond from this place.

Over the next several weeks, Steve noticed he was not reacting to his colleague's glares, silent judgements, awkward conversations, avoidance, and uncomfortable silences around the office and during meetings. He didn't have to take on their projections. There was worry and concern as he had a family to feed, but he didn't participate as much in the stories he was telling himself. He felt more grounded and aware. In fact, he even felt strong enough to be much more direct in the investigative meetings, suggesting their error was in their inability to keep records and that they had lost the receipts he submitted. He shared with me that he was feeling like a "steady presence."

Eventually, the situation was resolved. The receipts were found at the home of an employee in finance, who was working remotely. Looking back at it now seems quite hilarious, but in the moment, it is an entirely real and shaky situation. Steve and I were both relieved, and I could tell this event had left him changed in a deep way. Although he felt the mental itch to scream, "I told you so!" to his superiors for all the unfounded accusations, he said, "Maybe you have learned something from this?" and left it at that.

This could have all gone in a different direction. We have no control over the direction life takes or what lessens we have to learn. The rhythms of life are so unpredictable, and we must be alert at all times. We never know when it is our turn to be cast into the darkness of life, but we can't forsake our awareness for a self-image or public opinion; doing so places us right back into the state of separateness and suffering. As Awareness, we remain like a glacial mountain, unmoved.

In the next part, I describe the third phase of the moon cycle – the full moon, where we will explore the realms of death, grief and loss, and hellish experiences from a nondual perspective.

Part 5 – Full Moon Fever: Facing Death, Grief, Hell, and Nonbeing

The full moon, also known as the dark side of the moon, is the third main phase of the lunar cycle and represents a time of daemonic influences, heightened ego activity, and spiritual and mental distress. There is both a transcendent beauty and darkness in this phase of the moon cycle. Popular culture has linked the full moon to "driving people crazy" and a time of wild intensity. Some cultures like Buddhism believe the full moon exerts a pull on the mind, influencing one's personal unconscious and allowing it to rise to the surface of awareness and have full reign for the evening. One's fears, desires, and unresolved shadow issues take flight, often rendering one confused, lost, and fearful. It is a time when all of our hidden darkness is suddenly illuminated and our behaviors become unpredictable.

In this section, the full moon represents the encounter and transformation of some darker aspects of human consciousness found on the journey of awakening. The dark side of the moon lurks within some of the most terrifying and difficult encounters many people have to face when waking up from the dream of separation. Here, we begin by exploring the vulnerability and transforming power of accepting the completion of each moment when facing a horrific death and the loss of a loved one, followed by realizing that in a such an experience lies the essence of nondual being. We then move into the terrifying encounter of suddenly finding one's self in a hell realm of addiction, death, and nonbeing, and conclude with a radical acceptance of grief and loss, which serves as a possible gateway to awakening.

Chapter 1: Every Moment is Complete as It is: A Rolodex of Transformation and Release

Often times it's only suffering that wakes us up.

- P. T. Mistlberger

It has been pointed out repeatedly that the healing essence of awakened truth lies in our darkest experiences in life. In our most terrifying and painful moments – right at the heart of our grief and pain – exists the ultimate medicine of Nondual Being. That which can never be destroyed or changed is ever present in the midst of all human experiencing. Opening up to this realization brings about a radical shift in how we experience pain and suffering, transforming our perception from self-obsession to an awakened awareness. Whether we are lying on our deathbeds or kneeling down at the bedside of a dying loved one, existence always invites us to realize the truth of our situation and rest in the deathless and stateless state of who we are.

Brian Theriault

In September 2015, my wife and I entered what was to be the last few weeks of her life. For the previous year and a half, we climbed and descended the peaks and valleys of living with brain cancer and embracing a transformational journey. Nadine met her situation with the grace of love and surrender. She didn't want to "battle cancer," but rather, she opted to cooperate with it, which facilitated ease in letting go of life and in the possibility of realizing that which never dies. Her journey reminded me of the following Zen story:

I know you are very ill. Like a good Zen student, you are facing that sickness squarely. You may not know exactly who is suffering, but question yourself: What is the essence of this mind? Think only of this. You will need no more. Covet nothing. Your end which is endless is as a snowflake dissolving in the pure air.[xxxv]

Nadine and I were mirrors for each other. Her *beingness* was often ahead of her understanding, and she would frequently intuit the formless state of awareness beyond words, prior to her body and mind, and prior to the disease that consumed it. The outside world fell away effortlessly and all of our energy was focused on letting go of attachments, fears and desires, and fully surrendering to the dying process. Even though her body was riddled with cancer and disintegrating, Nadine's awareness and spark of life remained untouched; the absolute presence of who and what she was remained vibrant and clear. As she approached the last few days of her life, she carried no fear in her heart, and she shared with me that she was ready to go.

For the entire evening before her death, I spoke to her about our life together, of the love and surrender she mirrored to me. I told her I loved her. Nothing was left unsaid. My words felt vulnerable and clear. I knew death was imminent, and I did not want to waste our final moments together on unnecessary words. I was highly conscious of what I said and the way I said it. I did not want to create confusion in her or cause her to grasp onto the body as she was preparing to leave. If she felt ready, I told her it was okay to leave that evening; I told her I was okay, and she could continue her journey knowing that everything was completed here. We all loved her deeply.

I felt so exhausted. Around ten-thirty that evening, Nadine slipped into a coma and her panting breath was rapid. I decided to give her the midnight medication early, kissed her, and told her I loved her very much. I went to lie down in the other room and there, I felt the coldness of death throughout my being. I was so cold. My whole body was shivering. I turned the heat up in the house, but I still felt frozen. I simply couldn't rest. I got up to check on her, and noticed she had passed away.

A thundering silence filled the room. The coldness of death was her way of letting me know she had gone. It is common for the dying to wait until their loved ones have left the room before leaving the body. I immediately went to her bedside and whispered in her ear, telling her it was okay to let go and okay to leave, to trust what was happening to her and cooperate with her journey as she had in this life. I encouraged her to look for any helpful presence or beings that might guide her. I told her to go with them and repeated that I loved her. As I sat down on the couch facing our front living-room window, a star shot across the sky, lighting up the night. I smiled, thinking to myself, '*What a beautiful way to leave this world.*' It was such a beautiful death.

It was soon after her passing that the pendulum of release and transformation swung my way like a huge wrecking ball of energy. The next morning, with the few hours I had slept, I woke up to a profound silence and stillness throughout the house. Nadine's body had been taken away in the early hours of the morning, and the house was empty of all activity. The house looked like an empty emergency room. The energy of my routine over the last two years was still in the "on" position; I was ready to deliver medications, change bedsheets, and prepare breakfast, but then there was nothing that needed to be done. I sat on the couch for a few hours simply riding this accumulated energy. A charged energy ran through everything in the room. The palliative bed, pictures, syringes, and the clothing; everything carried a frequency supported by memory, association, feeling, and thought. It was intense. The residual events of the last two years were still very much active in the room and within my being. I eventually left the house and went for a walk.

For three full days, I was plunged into intense feelings of vulnerability and sadness. A flood of sensations, emotions, associations, images, and memories surged through my being each day. The mind was actively engaged in replaying images of our time together. The last several months had left an energetic imprint on my being, and I knew enough to simply allow space for this act of replaying frozen moments in time. It felt like a Rolodex of images would pass through my mind, with a few key images continually repeating themselves. I would surrender to their force and allow the energy to roll through me, discharging all the excess accumulated vitality. Waves of sadness and grief would fill my being and seemingly release themselves. But this relief was only temporary.

The mind would cycle through itself once again, replaying familiar scenes of sadness and love from our journey together. The living room of our home, where Nadine spent her final days, held so much energy that the mere sight of the medical equipment and furniture triggered a flood of emotions. It would be more than a week before the palliative home care team picked up the bed and medical supplies. Naturally, it was difficult to spend much time in the home. I went for long walks in the community and continued to stay with each emotion and each image meditatively as they arose and moved through me. For three days, it felt like my being was going through an intense and repeated purging process.

On the third evening, I visited with Nadine's sister and her family, believing this would provide some reprieve, but I failed to realize that her home also carried a similar energetic charge. Nadine and I had spent a lot of time together there, visiting her family and playing with our niece. As I sat at the dinner table, my situation reached a crescendo; a massive surge of energy raced through my being, once again accompanied by the felt presence of the essence of Nadine in the room. In fact, both her sister and I could see Nadine walking across the living room floor to the couch where she often sat. I became emotional and headed for the bathroom.

It was there, spontaneously, that the wrecking ball of release finally hit me. As I filled a cup with water, the flood of images began to race through my mind at an increasingly greater speed than before. The Rolodex of images would rapidly flash through my mind's eye, pausing momentarily on a select few before repeating itself. Without my involvement, something had changed. When the reel finally paused on an image, I saw, in that particular frame, a fragment of my consciousness that was still actively involved. I was still dynamically engaged in each image, which kept it fully alive and fully charged! I was stunned; I realized that not only did I need to be with this process in a place of no judgement, but I also had to recognize that within each image, the moment itself was complete; I had to see the completeness of each moment, no matter what was happening in that particular view. The vision of Nadine's lifeless, raw body lying on the palliative bed held the most charge.

There was sadness and grief mixed with a racing set of memories of a wonderful life lived together. The first moment we met, our jokes and shared sense of humour, moving into our home, camping trips, and our time traveling in Europe. It all manifested in my awareness. Each scene was relived the moment I became fixated on it. In the image of me gazing at Nadine's lifeless body, I recognized, from this witnessing position, that a fragment of my consciousness was still there: making sure everything was okay, ensuring the body was in the proper position and being taken care of; trying to close her eyelids (which they wouldn't); and saying the correct things. Essentially, this fragment of my consciousness was stuck trying to ensure Nadine was given the "proper goodbye." As this image left, a new one would take its place, and again, I observed a fragment of my consciousness still actively participating in a frozen moment in time.

What happened next proved transformative. As my mind cycled back to the familiar set of images, my awareness went into each view and realized the completeness of the moment. It released itself by itself, with no effort or mental strategy, and with the recognition that each moment was complete. This was a non-verbal realization that continued with each frame that presented itself. It would move into the heart of the image and announce its completeness. Each image fell away, and the associated charge dissipated. I was shocked! Everything was happening automatically. The awareness kept going into various visions and releasing the pent-up energy that was still operating in each image. I started to feel light and free. The pain and suffering vanished. The undercurrent of that which never dies felt incredibly light. The release was in seeing that there is no one that dies; there is no one that dies, fundamentally; yet, there appears to be. There is no one, no little independent self that is grieving either; yet, there is sadness. All of it, the whole experience was a dramatic event taking place in Awareness.

It was all an act of grace and divine will. Grace appears when we are not there, when we have ceased being a separate self. When we are an opening – ripe and ready to receive – grace arrives, showing us the truth of our situation. It happens without our involvement.

It showed me, clearly, how thoroughly we are not in control of this Divine process. Life happens on its own accord and likewise reveals the mysteries of existence on its own consensus.

I do not know how much time passed. It felt like time did not play a role in this revelation. It was an event outside of time and space. As I left the bathroom and returned to the dinner table, I looked around my sister-in-law's house and noticed the absence of the energetic charge and the presence of Nadine. There was clarity and spaciousness in the room and within my soul. My sister-in-law noticed something had happened, but I did not share the details of my experience.

When I arrived home that evening, I thought I would be overwhelmed. I entered the living room and observed the medical equipment; nothing. 'This is strange,' I thought. I even lay down on the palliative bed for a while, trying to summon the vanished images and feelings. And nothing still. I felt a tremendous sense of peace and surrender. I conjured images of Nadine and felt no traumatic energy. However, I could feel a pervasive love throughout my being. The next day, I continued to test this realization, lying on the palliative bed and cleaning up the medical supplies. Again, nothing. I fell into a trusting space with this realization and allowed it to permeate my being. This trust was a gift from existence, and I am forever grateful.

Over the next few days, I contemplated what had happened and identified a few insights. Incomplete moments create karma and the ongoing cycles of birth and death. Whatever remains incomplete in our consciousness keeps us on the wheel of life and death. I recognized that each vision I experienced seemed to hold its very own world, populated with people, places, and things, and was subject to the mercy of the laws of existence. Each image and each world was held in an infinite space, and the moment I became fixated on the dynamics of one of those pictures, I became a self amongst other selves, navigating the ups and downs of that particular moment. Not seeing the moment as complete facilitated the emergence of a self/other dualism and the world of pain and suffering. The psychologist, Stephen Wolinsky, experienced a similar realization in his own meditative practice:

> *I did not know why these bubble-universes appeared or disappeared in this strange and yet familiar abyss. A bubble-universe-realm would appear and then disappear and then another bubble-universe-realm appeared out of the emptiness. For example, inside one bubble was the concept of birth and death. At first I laughed because **as the emptiness** there was no such thing as birth or death. Soon however if or as I merged through this membrane-bubble and actually became this bubble-universe so it was true.*[xxxvi]

In seeing the completeness of each moment and not identifying with pervading, transient images and thoughts, awareness releases us from the dualistic notions of the self/other and life/death paradigms. As sentient beings, we are involved in an eternal process of constant transformation. This has always been the case. Today, there is a profound sense of peace that permeates my being; one I have never experienced before. The seriousness of life has left my consciousness, and I feel free and more and more at ease. Nadine's final gift showed me how one lives her life is how one will live her death. And so, with an open heart, the moment is received and met with the light of Awareness, where there exists no division, separation, or sense of incompleteness. Instead, there is *just this*.

Chapter 2: The Moon in the Gutter: Transforming the Terror of a Horrifying Death Experience

At the heart of the most intense suffering, right at the heart of it, there is simply nobody there who suffers. Even suffering is pointing to the absence of the separate, solid person. And that can be very difficult to hear.

- Jeff Foster

There was a time when I was intrigued by reading stories about spiritual teachers and gurus experiencing a graceful death. I was fascinated to read how there was such ease and fluidity in their ability to let go of the body and mind. No complaints, no worries, just a fluid surrender into eternity. There are numerous stories describing gurus, wherein the final moments of their life, are surrounded by their loving devotees eagerly waiting to receive the final teaching or the last transmissional blast of awakening. Some gurus would rhyme off a Zen-like Haiku poem and expound original never heard before nondual wisdom prior to taking their last breath. Others would simply offer a nonverbal gesture and be done with it.

At the time, I thought this was a hallmark of spiritual awakening. I used to envision having such an experience on my deathbed, surrounded by loving friends and family, where I'm about to deliver some witty nondual one liner before checking out. I even entertained the image of being carted away to have the body burned on a funeral pyre, like they would do in India. It didn't take long before my spiritual fantasy blew up. All I had to do was read the newspaper or simply turn on the TV to witness the horrific deaths people endured in everyday life. I would hear about famous spiritual teachers being randomly killed in car accidents, robbed and beaten, or simply dropping dead of a heart attack. There was nothing graceful about it. It was all just happening. They were dying ordinary deaths, taking place in the gutters of life. It was raw and real, completely unpredictable, and even gruesome at times. It was becoming obvious to me that my fascination about achieving a graceful death was all a mind-made spiritual fantasy, another mental strategy in self-survival, and need for being remembered or immortalized in some special way. And furthermore, it was a defense mechanism against the awful truth of death; that it can be brutal, messy, unforgiving, and terrifying. We have no control over it, yet the mind will go to great lengths to secure a comfortable death in time. It's all a grand illusion, though, and we must go beyond the limited view of identifying with the body and mind. Existence decides what happens except, who we are, remains uninvolved. This requires us to face our fear and terror of a brutal death.

Several years ago, a horrifying tragedy struck my community, which forced me to address the terror that had been percolating in my being for many years. It was a tragedy that continues to reverberate in the collective psyche today and made national headlines all over the world. While travelling home on a Greyhound Bus one evening, a young man was savagely attacked by another passenger, who wielded a massive hunting knife and was experiencing a schizophrenic psychosis. Neither of them knew each other. The young man was simply sitting in his seat, with his headphones on and listening to music, while his attacker savagely beheaded him. There was total chaos and madness on the bus. It all happened quite spontaneously and within a few minutes. The bus came to a halt as all the other passengers quickly exited before a huge police force ended the situation.

There was something about his tragic death that ignited a deep desire in me to face my own terror and find a resolution to it. We need to encounter our terror in order to pass through it. While sitting at my kitchen table, I was so shocked reading about his death that it sent familiar waves of terror racing throughout my own being. Waves upon waves of fear and energy suddenly manifested throughout my whole body, and I felt like I was spiralling into a vortex of fear. A series of images, sensations, and feelings flashed before my eyes, and I started to sweat profusely. It felt like my own terror of an imagined horrific death was ignited and stayed with me for a period of time. It seemed to be an undercurrent in my being demanding attention. Over the next few days, I realized the dread and horror were linked to a frozen moment in time I had not yet resolved.

One evening, while reading, I recalled the moment. I was about eight-years-old and on vacation with my family in Florida when one day, while playing in the ocean close to the shore, I was suddenly pulled underwater by a rip current. One moment I was collecting seashells and driftwood, and the next, I was physically spiralling into the depths of the ocean. I was in total shock and terror; I had no idea what was happening. I couldn't breathe, and I had no control whatsoever. Everything was happening so fast. All I could see were bubbles and blue blackness as I was pulled further and further out into the ocean. I was so terrified; I thought I was going to die. And then suddenly, I popped up to the surface like a cork bobbing in the ocean; I was shocked and stunned. I had no idea what was happening, and then I felt a great deal of fright when I noticed just how far out into the ocean I had been pulled. I could see people running down the beach yelling at me to swim to shore. A burst of fear exploded inside me as I thought they were screaming that a shark was swimming towards me, so I frantically swam to shore. The movie poster of Jaws kept flashing through my mind as I screamed and flailed about, trying to swim to shore. I had never felt such terror like that before. Although I made it to safety and was attended to, the energy of that dread continued to haunt me as an adult.

While sitting in my chair, the imagery flashed through my awareness at an accelerating rate. I could feel a familiar terror race through my being, igniting intense feelings and sensations. I could feel a great deal of heat in my body, and I was beginning to sweat heavily. Instead of keeping the experience at bay, though, I felt guided in staying open to it. I was very aware of what was happening. There was an understanding taking place. I let myself re-experience the traumatic event in its entirety. I saw myself as a child in total confusion and fear, descending into the depths of the ocean, and struggling to survive. Immediately, I saw a picture of a clenched fist in my consciousness, and I simultaneously felt it in my guts. Like the vision of my eight-year-old self, I was still stuck in survival mode as an adult, hanging tightly, and struggling to survive. I then experienced an intuitive feeling sense that this had been a big pattern which played out in my adulthood; the desire and attachment to the body, existence, and life itself. I seemed to be in a constant state of survival mode. This also appeared to play a big role in influencing the decisions I made in my life and the ways in which I was being in the world. As this was revealed to me, I felt a spontaneous sense of letting go and unclenching of the fist and knot of selfhood. It was not an act of effort but one of realization and understanding. The clenched fist suddenly relaxed, and I felt a great deal of release and freedom running through me. I could see the terror I had been carrying in my soul was fuelled by my desire to exist as a separate self. The fear of an awful death ran through me, but now something had shifted. The terror and panic were there, but my stance towards it had dramatically changed. I stopped seeing my experience as being a problem or something terrible that shouldn't be happening. It was the strangest yet revealing experience I had ever felt. It was like I had passed through the vortex of my own terror and evaporated into nothingness. The moment I accepted my terror, the imagined horrific death scenarios I entertained dissolved, and freedom was found. In some ways, my experience reminded me of Adyashanti's method of dealing with unresolved past-life traumas. Although I wasn't experiencing a past-life event, the process seemed similar:

There were certain confusions, fears, hesitations, and doubts that were unresolved in particular lifetimes. In certain lifetimes, what was unresolved was a feeling of confusion about what happened at the time of death. In one lifetime, I drowned and did not know what was happening, and there was tremendous terror and confusion as the body disappeared into the water. Seeing this lifetime and the confusion at the moment of death, I immediately knew what I had to do. I had to rectify the confusion and explain to the dream of me that I died, that I fell off a boat and drowned. When I did this, all of a sudden the confusion from that lifetime popped like a bubble, and there was a tremendous sense of freedom.[xxxvii]

I could see and undo my own dread in this particular life by simply allowing it to be there and understanding its nature. When

I allowed myself to pass through the experience, the accumulated energy resolved itself. I was no longer struggling to hold on. At the heart of terror exists the healing essence of nondual being. By letting go of my need to survive, I re-awakened a deeper truth found in the midst of our most terrifying experiences. There is no one there at the heart of our own darkness. There is simply no separate little "me" to survive or to even be killed. It was so clear to me. There is no centre that can be destroyed because we do not exist as a formless point in space and time. We are the vast, timeless, and spaceless opening of truth now, no matter what is happening. There can be fear and panic, horror and excruciating pain, but none of it is seen as a problem anymore. We tend to our pain while knowing at a deep level that there is no one who is impacted by it. We no longer try to get rid of pain and suffering. There is no need to transcend the fear or to manipulate our experience, and there is no judgement; there is just the raw reality of what is happening at the moment, with the clear recognition that it is all happening to no one in particular. We are not avoiding life, and we are not attempting to secure a future for ourselves. We are in such a state of *let-go*, hanging loose in the body and mind, surrendering to each moment, and not holding on. The identification with the body is relaxed, and we can drop it at any time. The need to survive in form has disappeared as we have surrendered our identifications. We are life itself and plugged into eternity, whether we are embodied or not. The terror of death only exists in the mind and perpetuates the existence of the separate self.

This was the key I had been missing for so long and failed to embody in my everyday life. In fact, this was the insight being pointed to by all the dying spiritual teachers and gurus I had read about so long ago, and yet totally missed. I got lost in the fantasy of a graceful death, reading all the stories, and missed the key transformational insight, that at the heart of death, no matter how it happens, there is simply no one there. There is no solid self who lives or dies, no matter how terrible or horrifying the experience may be.

This experience transferred into my clinical work with clients. Sometimes, in my therapeutic work with clients, who reported experiencing a pronounced fear of a horrifying death, I would invite them to imagine themselves in their projected scenario. I'd instruct them to fully experience it, in the here and now, as a means of moving through it and perhaps grasping the underlying truth of who they are. It made no sense for me to simply tell them that their story of a horrifying death was just that, a story; this simply didn't address the huge, overwhelming and horrific energy lurking within. By guiding clients to live through the imagined terror without judging it or compartmentalizing it, it seemed to serve as a window of opportunity for them to experience that which is beyond life and death altogether.

I remember one particular individual whom I worked with a few years ago, Rob, who loved touring the countryside while riding his motorcycle but carried a fear of being mangled up in an accident. I instructed him to allow the imagery and experience to play itself out in his mind's eye and to fully see himself going through it. While sitting in his chair, he experienced the energy, feelings, sensations, and imagery; he saw his body torn apart and mangled on the side of the highway. He played through the event as if he was dying now. It was as though he was embracing a death energy in the room, letting go of his body, and moving through the terror. After some time, Rob shared feeling a calm presence and stillness as the vision of his imagined motorcycle accident unfolded before him. He could connect with the witnessing presence of his being and could feel into the ok-ness of the experience; to see it as another event in time and relax into it, fully surrendered. It's okay to simply let go and drop into the ocean of existence.

It seems paradoxical, but unless we pass through our feelings of terror and experience nonbeing, we cannot fully come to live an awakened life. The fear is a result of not knowing how to be empty or to embrace nothingness and nonbeing at the core of our beings. When we allow and accept the fear and horror in our lives, we are paradoxically free from it. In the gutters of life exists the potential of waking up to the moonlight of our own awareness.

Chapter 3: Revisiting Jacobs Ladder: Addiction, Hell, and You

> *The only thing that burns in Hell is the part of you that won't let go of life, your memories, your attachments. They burn them all away. But they're not punishing you ... They're freeing your soul. So, if you're frightened of dying and ... and you're holding on, you'll see devils tearing your life away. But if you've made your peace, then the devils are really angels, freeing you from the earth.*
>
> - Luis, Jacob's Ladder

Jacob's Ladder, an intense movie, describes non-ordinary states of consciousness and hellish experiences at the moment of death. The Biblical story of the prophet Jacob and his visionary dream of ascending a ladder stretching towards Heaven, becomes a metaphor for transforming human consciousness at the moment of death. In the movie, Jacob (played by Tim Robbins) suffers a fatal wound during the Vietnam War, and we see doctors frantically working to save his life. The movie quickly shifts to what appears to be Jacob's life during the post-war era. Here, we see him attempting to reconcile the trauma of being wounded in the war, while also dealing with the loss of his young son, difficult relationships, and unresolved fears and desires. The death of his son is the most difficult experience for Jacob to work through, and when he reaches a place of acceptance, we see him climbing a staircase towards a brightly lit room, presumably Heaven (Truth). The movie is filled with nightmarish visions and images and distortions in time and space as Jacob's consciousness struggles to find peace and resolution. The final scene circles back to where the doctors are working on Jacob and finally declaring him dead. The movie ends with one of the doctors commenting on the strange smile spread across Jacob's face. In order to find peace, he had to work through his personal demons and unresolved life experiences. His Hell was of his own making.[xxxviii]

At some point in the course of our own spiritual transformations, we must go beyond the conventional view of Hell as being separate from our current existence. We must take responsibility and recognize that we are the architects of our own demise. Hell is a self-created realm, designed and built out of our belief in self-separateness and division. The more we engage in self-serving acts and self-indulgences, the more we furnish a personalized *hellish environment*. Hell is a self-reflected conditioned state of the mind rooted in our unaddressed fears and desires, attachments, and confusions.

Our state of mind now determines the next moment. Any incomplete moments we carry in our being – all the accumulated addictions and unconscious impulses running wild at the depths of our soul – the whole karmic load of self-centeredness we carry – all will eventually come screaming to the surface of our consciousness, seeking our attention the moment the body and mind are dropped. Adi Da put it quite succinctly:

> *When you die and the body drops off, mind makes you. After death, you live in the world of mind as you have created it while alive. The after-death states have been called 'bardos,' or 'planes.' Really, all such concepts are simply descriptions of how the mind operates dissociated from physical embodiment. You will spontaneously, through no will of your own, enter into realms of mind after death that correspond to your state of mind – not just your thinking mind but your subconscious and unconscious mind, the whole force of your tendency toward objects and conditional states. ... They are hells, purgatories, dark passages. They seem to go on for vast periods of time, even until they exhaust themselves and you pass out of them as you pass from one dream to the next.*[xxxix]

The mind can buffer our unprocessed psychological material only for so long before we have to face it. After death, we no longer have the psychological and physical means of keeping such repressed material at bay. We will be magnetically pulled to face and process it until released. We will be pulled this way and that based upon our fears and desires.

As depicted in Dante's *Inferno* and *The Tibetan Book of the Dead*, anything we have not processed in our lives which we have left repressed in our unconsciousness, will become our personal torment. Buddhist cosmology describes multiple levels of Hell, including boiling cauldrons, frozen landscapes, and torturous devices. These are not necessarily precise depictions of what to expect but metaphors for a particular range of experiences that can be found after death. Even human existence is considered an after-life experience and can represent a Hell realm for many individuals.

Brian Theriault

Entering a Post-Operative Hell Realm

Not too long ago, while at the hospital with my wife, who was undergoing major brain surgery, I found myself in my own Hell realm. Not only did I witness other beings experiencing and struggling with their own nightmares, but also found myself having to address some of my own. The moment I walked through the doors of the recovery room to visit my wife, who had just finished the surgery, I was immediately transported into what I would later describe as a *post-operative Hell realm*. The room was full of chaos and madness. It was a large, oval room with no windows and fourteen beds filled with patients who had just finished major surgery. One patient was screaming gibberish and flailing about like a wounded animal. He appeared to be stuck in an animalistic existence, defecating himself and screaming nonsense. On the other side of the room, an elderly woman was moaning about not wanting to die. She wept and wept with family and friends by her side, reaching for life, and seemingly unable to let go. The desire for life was so strong. Another individual was in a fit of anger, yelling at the nurses, and demanding they tend to his every need. He seemed to be raging against existence. There were various other patients who appeared to be locked in catatonic states and looked strangely like earthbound apparitions just on the threshold of life and death. They seemed frozen in a state of non-response and unable or unwilling to participate in their own recovery.

And then, a tidal wave of chaotic energy hit and plunged me into states of shock and confusion. As I arrived at my wife's bedside, I noticed myself quickly contracting and tensing up, wanting to shield Nadine from all the perceived intensity and chaos in the room. Suddenly, the young woman beside Nadine flat-lined, and the nurses and doctors rushed to bring her back to life. My contractions increased, unknowingly feeding my own fear and terror. I would not realize this until early the next morning, and the more defensive I became toward the event, the more I plunged into a difficult and terrifying form. My initial state of contraction kick-started my trip down the *Highway to Hell*. I became divided and separate from everything and everyone in the room. In many ways, like the elderly woman weeping that she did not want to die, I too was grasping at life, attempting to hold on and defend against existence. I saw this place as terrible. I spent the rest of the day in and out of a form of confusion, trying to ground and make sense of my experience while Nadine slept.

Later that evening, as I slept, I was plagued with horrible nightmares and terrifying imagery. I was chased by demonic figures who jumped and hid, surrounded me, and tried to capture me; I ran and ran down a long hallway, opening one door after another, only to find myself back in the same black hallway, being chased by the same visions. I was still holding on to the desire for life and looking for a better outcome; I failed to realize how I had set myself up the previous day when I contracted around the chaos in the post-op recovery room. What made my experience hellish was my desire to escape it. This was key. My projected desire to protect and shield Nadine from the turmoil, which carried on throughout the day, made the whole event terrifying. I wanted things to be different. The energy and desire for escape fuelled the demonic chases that presented in my dreams. The moment I adopted a defensive posture in the recovery room is the moment I simultaneously created a perceived threat. All it took was the smallest of clenching in my being. I was shocked by my discovery.

> Whenever and wherever your mind is caught in miseries and pain, recognize at once that there is some foolishness on your part in interpreting the manifest Brahman. You believe unavoidables are avoidables; your miseries begin from the very point of the belief. You hope that that which is destined to happen may not happen, and at this point your worries begin; anguish and unease are created. No, what is to happen will happen. There is no escape from it, nothing else can happen. When you accept this mantra, when you accept this arrangement of the manifest Brahman totally, everything within you will become calm and quiet. Then there is nothing to worry you.[xl]

I spent a part of the morning contemplating my situation. I took some time to meditate and relax the mental activity I was engaged in, and it started to dawn on me just how I was creating my own misery. I traced its origin to the moment I walked into the post-op recovery room. I could see myself solidify around the experiences taking place in the room. I felt hardened, but in seeing this, the feeling released itself. The moment I did not run from my experience, the tightening started to disappear and lose its energetic charge. I experienced a felt sense of purging the accumulated energy I had unwittingly stored inside myself the previous day. Hell burns itself up the moment we realize there is no escape. It was a paradoxical and experiential felt insight.

Although tired and exhausted, I felt my heart expand, and I experienced a lightness in my being. I met with Nadine early that morning, and together we sat with open hearts and receiving presence. The same level of chaos was present, however, I did not see it as a problem anymore. Instead, I felt a deeper level of compassion that allowed me to meet and receive the experiences in an undefended way. My mind would attempt to contract around a particular experience, but I would simply not engage, and it quickly disappeared. The moment I followed a train of thought, I could feel the clenching develop. In observing this, I could choose to be with Nadine and the energy in the room in a more undivided way. These insights were gifts, and they became integral to my being now and in the last months my wife and I had together. My new revelations on ways of being in a *hellish environment* were some things I wanted to share with the people I work with in my counselling practice.

Bill's Journey

I had the opportunity to work with Bill, who had been battling an internet and video pornography addiction for many years. It was wreaking havoc in his life. Although he was experiencing some success in freeing himself from the shackles of addiction, he found himself easily relapsing when under stress. His marriage was beginning to fall apart. Bill had worked hard to try and overcome his addiction, but late one night it became unbearable, and he sadly took his own life. I was so devastated to learn of his passing. There was neither prior history of suicidal thoughts nor any indication that he was in this particular state of mind. It would take me many months to process his loss and review the work we had engaged in together.

Several months after his death, Bill's partner, Paul, scheduled a counselling session with me, wanting to explore some unusual experiences he had been having since his passing. When we met, Paul seemed anxious and upset. I expected we would engage in some form of grief work, however, what he shared with me became a journey into his deceased partner's Hell realm. He described that since his death, he would see him wandering around in the house, visibly angry and upset. He would even see him late at night, sitting on the couch in the living room, frustrated and agitated, looking for the TV remote control, yet never being able to find it. While alive, this was his pattern of acting out, where late at night, while Paul was asleep, he would secretly engage in his addictive behavior and order pornographic movies. Paul wept, feeling lost and confused, and even began questioning his own sanity.

Bill's situation was similar to the Buddhist Hell realm of *the hungry ghost*, which is a well-known metaphor used today to describe unresolved cravings and addictions. Alive or dead, individuals locked in this state are depicted as demon-like creatures tormented by unfulfilled desires and fixations, demanding the impossibility that they be fulfilled. Their desires are fuelled by their past karmic conditioning. They wander like fiends, lifeless and hell-bent on feeding their cravings. Some *hungry ghosts* find they can eat, but no food is available; others are trapped in large halls with rows of buffet tables full of food, but they have pinhole mouths and cannot swallow. A ghost can spend a large amount of time in this realm until the mind either exhausts itself or wisdom is achieved.

Paul and I spent several sessions together normalizing his experiences and helping his late husband's consciousness move on through communication and meditative techniques. I recalled my own hellish events at the hospital, and invited him to resist escaping his situation or doubting his experiences. They challenged his rational mind, so we worked on discarding mental conclusions about what he was witnessing, and instead, focussed on trusting his experiences and perceptions. I also encouraged him to communicate these insights to his husband's consciousness in a way that felt right for him. Also, I urged Paul to communicate with Bill and tell him he had died, and that he was actively engaging in his addictive patterns in an attempt to find release. He was invited to totally surrender to his dilemma, not to fight it, or to follow through on chasing his yearnings. It was a means of inviting Bill to see desire as simply energy, which he did not need to actively chase. By allowing the wanting to race through our consciousness without grabbing it, the possibility of release and freedom can be found. As Bill was familiar with these concepts from our previous work together, I felt this would be beneficial.

Eventually, Paul did report that the experiences had stopped, but it was never quite clear whether Bill was released from his addiction. Nonetheless, it was clear that lust and desire had become his Hell realm. All we can do is surrender and accept where it is that we happen to find ourselves. Death is not necessarily a release from our pain and longing. Everything is accounted for and is due to our own making.

Whatever we are attracted to in the moment becomes our reality. If we remain fixated on the images, thoughts, and experiences that flash before us upon death, we whirl in the stream of fear and desire. We are seemingly at the mercy of our own fixations. Letting go of and relaxing our mental fixations while alive and being accustomed to the spacious emptiness from which they arise, frees us from the limits that can enclose us when exiting the body. This work can be done now. We can feel into what is driving our sense of self and personality. We can glean from where in our being we are operating from, through reflection and open-ended inquiry. There is a possibility of becoming clear in our souls and honing in on what we need to work on by asking ourselves some pointed questions: *'What am I still attached to at this moment? Am I carrying any pain? How is it that I'm creating my own Hell now? What are my fears? What are my desires?'*

We can surrender to what is revealed to us and trust in its own natural unfolding process. If we do not allow our consciousness to be swept away by the mind, we start uncovering the deeper, spacious presence of who we are. We begin anchoring ourselves here, in spaceless awareness, where we can effortlessly observe the mechanics of our mental functioning. The desire for self-identity and the fear of anything that challenges our position becomes our personal nightmare. As our wisdom grows, we start to peel away layer upon layer of the mind and arrive at an ever-increasing understanding; I am prior to the body and mind, so where is the question of bondage and the need for escape? The more we want to escape our situations, addictions, impulses, and unconsciousness, the more we feed and give them life. This also includes the desire to escape through ascension towards truth or a Heavenly experience. The desire for union or God itself facilitates the makings of a nightmare where we are endlessly in pursuit of something that exists only in the mind. It is simply thought chasing thought.

We cannot bypass any of this, and we need to be clear within our beings. We ascend and descend the ladder of consciousness – mental, emotional, physical, and spiritual – clearing out any fixations and confusions that continue to dominate us and leave us feeling separate and estranged from life. We have to be honest with ourselves and investigate where it is we are still caught, where in our beings we are still practicing self-separation. By doing this, we are unravelling the knots of our own confusion from this space of interconnected awareness. The mind no longer dominates our attention and energy. If we embrace the wisdom of no escape and accept our situation without resorting to the usual strategies of the mind, our experiences can transform themselves. When we stop giving our happenings energy through fear and desire, fear and desire begin to collapse on their own. What was once believed to be so frightening or so lustful thins out and disappears. The illusion collapses, and we return to our natural, effortless state of Being.

When we are abiding as truth, there is no separation; we are the pain, and we are the madness; we are the confusion and the Hellish experiences. Seeing that there is no cure for any of this, and that there never needed to be one in the first place, is the freedom and peace that is always already available.

Chapter 4: Radical Acceptance: Grief as a Gateway to Nondual Being

---

There was a man of Wei, Tung-men Wu, who did not grieve when his son died.

His wife said to him:
'No one in the world loves his son as much as you did, why do you not grieve now he is dead?'

He answered:
'I had no son, and when I had no son I did not grieve. Now that he is dead it is the same as it was before, when I had no son. Why should I grieve over him?'

- Taoist Story

This is not a tale of an emotionally disconnected father but of a man who is living an awakened life; a man, whom through a spontaneous act of grace, has made the shift in perception from that of a separate bound entity to a vastness beyond description. It is another parable pointing to the ineffable presence of who we are at this moment. Grief is an entirely appropriate response to the loss of a loved one. This is nothing about denying our humanness, but it is yet another invitation to go beyond self-identity and our typical orientation to grief and realize truth. Realizing the "Deathless state" requires us to drop out of our social games and ritualized forms of sorrow we have learned throughout our lives and see that death is not only taking place in the loss of our loved one but also within our own being. This chasm has to be crossed. Death is not over there happening to someone else; it is here and now. Death is reacted to, so grief and sorrow can become nothing more than a form of ritualized ego activity that has very little to do with the recently deceased loved one and much more to do with one's own fear of death and non-existence. We need to see through the self/other knot and embrace death here and now.

As we suspend the mind and stop participating with it, we come to see that at the heart of the matter is the fear of *no-self*. Grief mirrors our fear of non-existence. It's always there, just underfoot, and in everything we do. No matter how much we avoid it, this fear permeates our nature. The fear of nothingness is excruciating, and we avoid it at all costs, except at some point, we have to face it in order to realize the truth. And the only real way through it is to surrender and accept its existence. No judgement and no preference are the keys to transforming our fear. We have to step into the fire of fear and let it consume us fully. We need to let our self burn in the fire of our awareness. When our mental commentary towards the experience settles the posture of separateness, our fear of nonbeing begins to collapse. The more we trust this process, the more we dis-identify from the mind and see that at the heart of fear is the radical truth of who we are. This requires a radical acceptance of opening our heart up to grief and fear and not managing or manipulating it in any way. By allowing our experience to move through us, unimpeded, it reveals the deeper truth of existence. At the heart of fear and grief is a spacious loving presence.

Every Evening Comes the Moon

When we are not locked into the mind, we can examine grief in an entirely new way, where our losses become a transformational opportunity. There are some vivid examples of such transformations that have left a deep impression on me and have become a living invitation in my own journey through grief. For example, while plummeting into the depths of a broken heart after the loss of his beloved wife, Shamala, from the autoimmune disease of Lupus, it became clear to Kriben Pillay that instead of participating with the mind that so desperately wanted to re-establish its familiar world, he shifted his focus to the dilemma of death itself and began inquiring into the reality of the separate self.

Certainly there was the death of the person known as Shamala, but was there really such a permanent person? ... The blatant truth is that we construct the person in our minds from the raw material of the impressions given by the person's body-mind, which are always changing; when the body-mind is no longer we are really mourning the loss of our own self-creation.[xli]

Similarly, for Mariam Greenspan, the loss of her infant son was so gut-wrenching that the experience shattered her sense of self.

Dead, he was nakedly mine and altogether gone all in the same instant. Time stood still and the world fell silent. I was drawn into a vortex, and the self I knew was irreversibly shattered. What happened next: an energy larger than my body could contain broke through in a rush of strange, unfathomable syllables ... What came through me, as I stood and wrapped my arms around my dead baby, was a form of speech emanating from a source deeper than personality. Though utterly indecipherable, these strange sounds were a kind of prayer.[xlii]

And for George Bedard, after being told by his doctors he was dying from Leukemia and had only a few hours to live (later to be revealed as inaccurate information received by his doctor), he dissolved into the stateless state of nondual being.

> *That day, I entered a state between life and death, as my mind was drawn further and further away from my body. I gradually became aware of a boundless expanse of light, an endless moonlight, soothing and comforting. There was no sense of self or having a body. I had disappeared into limitless, birthless space. For what seemed to be an eternity, I had rested in a place I had never really left.*[xliii]

Our losses can become fertile ground for awakening. The raw and vivid encounter with death and non-existence has to be met in awareness for us to truly live a fulfilling and free life. Grief holds such a transformative opportunity, and it is something I point to in my work with counselling clients.

Laura's Journey

Laura, a successful forty-year-old yoga instructor, had recently participated in and completed several group therapy sessions with me, exploring post-addiction recovery issues. Although she had saved her life from the trenches of drug addiction seven years ago and transitioned into embracing a healthier lifestyle, she felt it was time to heal the wound of grief related to the death of her mother. She reported finding it difficult to be openly vulnerable with her friends and family, experiencing intrusive thoughts related to her mother's death several times a month, and subsequently felt depleted in energy. Since feeling connected to the spiritual approach towards healing and recovery in the group therapy sessions, she requested a one-to-one counselling session with me to explore this issue further.

It became clear to me that Laura was very close to her mother, and her death was a huge loss for her. Her mother had lost her battle with cancer while Laura was in her second year of recovery, and despite the amount of stress Laura felt at that time, she proudly shared being able to remain abstinent from drugs. Laura went on to describe how powerfully healing it was for her to be by her mother's bedside during the last few moments of her life but subsequently felt conflicted, stating that "It just wasn't her time, I know we all return to the Source, but she had so much left to give," she said.

I let this statement hang in silence for a few moments sensing that her judgement of "it wasn't her time" was a way in which she contracted upon herself and defended against death and the terror of nonbeing. I suspected that a large part of her soul was energetically stuck in the past of "there and then" rather than centered in the "here and now." Eckhart Tolle describes this condition as the pain-body where an accumulation of demands placed on experiences collects over time and lodges within one's being, stunting their ability to feel totally open and available in the moment.[xliv] It was as if her mother's death had become a frozen moment in time for her.

I wanted to point out to Laura how she was contracting upon herself through her story of how things should have turned out differently for her mother. I asked Laura to repeat the statements, "it just wasn't her time, and she had so much left to give," a few times slowly to herself and notice how her body-mind responded to it. As she did this, she mentioned feeling tightness and heaviness throughout her body and an inability to move. While teary-eyed, she followed up with a vivid image of herself standing in a graveyard surrounded by tombstones. I asked her to stay with her imagery and to describe it. "I see myself walking through the graveyard, but I can't find the gate to get out. I feel trapped," she said. I felt the moment held a transformational opportunity, so I invited Laura to "Rather than look for a way out, what would happen if you just accepted your situation as it is. That, in fact, there is no way out of this?" It is only when the mind is exhausted and gives up trying to figure it out, trying to save itself, and avoid its extinction, that the possibility of relaxing into nondual being takes place.

I could see her wrestling with this invitation. "I'm not sure what you mean," she stated. "Seeing yourself in the graveyard, can you allow yourself to relax the desire to save yourself here? What happens if you allow the realization that there is no gate?" I replied. After a few minutes, she was shocked to find that the imagery of the graveyard suddenly dissolved and revealed "an empty blankness, an empty space," as she called it. In astonishment, she shared, "Everything just went empty and blank. I can still see, but not as me, if that makes any sense?" She described it as terrifying and exhilarating all at the same time. I encouraged her to cooperate with her process and to dissolve into the intense energy of the "empty-blankness" without resisting it in any way. Seeing that the energy of nonbeing is always with us in every moment, I was curious to see if she could accept it, here and now, and let go of any attempt to save herself. "I feel a lot of fear in my heart, though," she worried. "Let fear have its place and just surrender to it," I instructed. I suspected Laura was perceiving the experience of emptiness as a negative one and something to be avoided. The fear of her own non-existence was evident. As I watched her process the situation, I observed a calmness overtake her as she relaxed more and more into her experience. With tears rolling down her eyes, she shared noticing the absence of fear and feeling as if she was held by what she referred to as an "imageless eternal mother."

In some ways, Laura's experience reminded me of the story of the Zen monk who, despite living a clean and morally ascetic life, was still tossed into the hell realm upon his death. Realizing his fate was sealed, and there was nothing he could do, he simply sat down and totally accepted the situation. Miraculously, the truth of his being spontaneously revealed itself through a deep acceptance.

I was still curious about the depth of her feelings and wanted to see if there were any residual demands placed upon the moment of her mother's death. I invited Laura to close her eyes and recall the last few moments she spent with her dying mother, to slowly re-play the event through her mind and see if there were any demands placed there. After several moments, she reported, "I see it all happening and I feel a lot of energy in my body, but I feel okay. I feel some sadness, but it's okay. I feel a lot of tingling sensations in my arms and legs as well, but it feels like a release." After a few minutes she continued, "I feel like a still calm lake, it's very peaceful." We spent the remainder of our session sitting in the absolute stillness of the moment, allowing the energy of life and death to pass through us in open awareness.

Even in the darkest of moments, our true being remains radiantly clear and transparent, unobstructed by the dramas of life. Grief and loss are seen to be another transformational opportunity to recognize that which is already here, and free us from the straitjacket of separation. As the next moment is never guaranteed, all we really have is the instance of this moment. And perhaps, in that instance, we can take the leap into the unknown, descend into the depths of the abyss of *no-self*, re-awaken to our primordial condition, and laugh at our desperate attempts to defend and save that which never really existed.

The next and last section of this book represents the final main phase of the moon cycle, which illustrates some of the problems found in spiritual transformation, transcendent experiences, devotional pursuits, and getting lost in the void.

Part 6 – The Last Quarter of Awakening: Popular Problems of a Spiritual Seeking Kind

The last quarter moon is now decreasing in illumination, and this is a time for deeper introspection and contemplative reflection. It is also a time for purging and letting go of anything that remains and obscures the realization of our true nature. Anything which does not serve the truth and abidance in nondual being needs to be seen through. Even after having dealt with one's personal pain, embracing an embodied awakened way of life, and working through the issues of grief, death, and nonbeing, there are problems that can continue to arise. The mind has a way of attaching itself to any and all kinds of experiences. One of the last points of self-referencing is in spiritual experiences and the nondual journey itself. The mind can take on a spiritual ego, attaching itself to spiritual teachers whereby one never stands on their own two feet, and forever chases non-ordinary blissful types of experiences. Now that the mind has let go of worldly desires, it now seeks out otherworldly pleasures. Therefore, the identification as a spiritual seeker needs to be addressed. The *seeker* needs to be seen through.

There are the common problems of defending against failure and defeat, difficulties in embracing the energy of absence, and suffering from a serious case of "Zen Sickness," in which one becomes completely lost in the empty formless aspects of existence, resulting in the inability to function in day-to-day living. It's easy to get caught up in the nondual community, thinking we are at the cutting edge of human consciousness, and special in our realizations and spiritual achievements. But we have to wake up out of everything, even the idea of awakening itself. Let's begin by looking at the devotional trap found with spiritual teachers.

Chapter 1: Untying the Devotional Knot of Suffering

We just can't seem to let go of our teachers, to stand alone without any authority and face life head-on, with no safety net.

- Jeff Foster

The guru is found within. All the spiritual teachers worth their salt have been pointing to this insight for centuries. Trust yourself and you will wake up to who and what you are. I am not suggesting there is no value in being devoted to a spiritual teacher or guru; many people have garnered tremendous insights, understandings and experienced many transformations in the company of their spiritual leader. What I am pointing to is the trap of dependency and an over-reliance on gurus at the expense of oneself. At the heart of this relationship, the teacher and devotee are one and the same. Nancy was another participant I interviewed for my master's thesis who realized this truth a number of years ago. While sitting alone one evening, she finally understood what was being pointed to:

And it broke, it just broke. I heard her, I got it. One day I realized Ammaji is telling me she's the same as me. She means she's the same. It's simple. It's a flat playing field. Everything is God! If everything is God, everything is God! And that includes the table. It includes the cement. It includes the garbage dump. It includes Hitler. It includes, you know, Bin Laden. It includes horror. It includes all the people I see in palliative care dying of horrible diseases for no reason that the mind will ever understand. Everything is God. Man, Brian, I'm telling you, it just blew the socks off me! It blew everything to smithereens! Just blew everything to smithereens![xlv]

There continues to be a huge phenomenon in the nondual world of seekers travelling around the world, devoting themselves to one spiritual teacher after another with the promise of being blown wide awake. Blind devotion breeds dependency. It's interesting to see that upon the death of their spiritual teacher, how many people who were once devoted to that particular guru, will swiftly jump into another spiritual community with another teacher and devote themselves, expecting that their "years of service" with their previous teacher grants them automatic inner inclusion.

Many people want their spiritual teachers to do all the work for them. They want the guru to give them the instant "transmissional" blast that will burn up all their accumulated karma. For some, they become addicted to the drama found in spiritual communities, the leader's charisma, and wanting to be within the inner circle. It's a drive to be mirrored, recognized, and seen as special in some way. It's a very dependent and adolescent way of living and viewed as a perpetually self-induced knot of suffering. I remember attending a week-long workshop with a well-known nondual teacher several years ago and being pushed aside by a group of people racing through the open doors to get a seat in the front row. I was shocked. It reminded me of when I crashed the gates to get to the front line of the stage at a rock concert. I sat down listening to the talk but observed the dynamics of dependency in the room, and more importantly, upon reflection, I saw how I had been a part of this in my own life. I saw my own form of dependence and reliance being played out. Many times, I wanted to be seen as being special, in tune with the group, and validated. I would turn to books, workshops, and close friends to help me and give me direction. It became a predictable routine until my friends caught on and encouraged me to simply sit in my pain and unease, confusion, and doubt. Our being becomes tangled up in the presence of the teacher, where we instantly lose access to our own understanding. We become so attached to the teacher that we never take the final step. Devotion to another serves as a vestige point for the self.

The story of the disciple Ananda learning of Buddha's imminent death is an example of this overreliance upon the guru. Ananda was on the verge of awakening, and for his entire life, he was at Buddha's side day in and day out, taking care of all his needs. The moment he learned Buddha was about to leave his body, he was overwhelmed and consumed with grief. He wailed and cried, and so much so, that there was now no way he was going to awaken. Buddha would soon be gone, and there was now no hope. Buddha deeply appreciated Ananda's love and support, but he knew his love of him was a barrier to his awakening. Seeing his pain, Buddha, filled with compassion and love, said to Ananda, "Be an island unto yourself, be your own refuge." Soon after Buddha's death, these words penetrated Ananda's heart, and he awakened.[xlvi]

It is important to see how we have set this whole game up for ourselves. We have to take some responsibility for having sold ourselves out. This was the case for Natalie, who contacted me, wishing to schedule several counselling sessions to address some problems she was having with her own spiritual teacher.

Natalie's Journey

Natalie was a middle-aged woman living in Thailand and had been involved with a spiritual community for well over fifteen years. She reported feeling angry and upset with how her guru was treating her; she didn't feel heard, understood, or validated in any way. Although Natalie benefitted greatly from the community, the last five years had been horrendous for her. She was always in conflict with her teacher, and she was often asked to leave the meditation hall where he was giving spiritual discourses. She claimed she wasn't being abusive towards her teacher, but she was also not one to hold back if she disagreed with something being said. In other words, she would challenge him on many points during his talks.

I smiled and said, "So you were interrupting his gig." She smiled and laughed. "Can you see this whole guru-disciple game as being one of the oldest dramas being played out in the spiritual journey?" I asked. "The disciple waiting to be recognized by the guru as being awakened and who can now join the ranks of a particular lineage is one of the oldest games out there," I added. It has even reached a point in some spiritual communities where teachers will declare themselves as the only awakened being throughout all time, even in the future. They become gatekeepers of existence, allowing or denying disciples entry into the ranks of the awakened. In the *Diamond Sutra*, one of the most important texts in Buddhism, it states, "The Absolute exalts the Holy person."[xlvii] It would be wise to meditate on this insight. The guru-disciple game can take on an extreme edge. A dependence on the guru supports the self/other stance, which allows the belief in the exclusive sense of the self to continue unabated.

Every Evening Comes the Moon

I asked Natalie if there was any truth to the possibility that she was orchestrating these conflicts as an attempt to try and take her teacher out as a means of being seen as bright and awakened like him. She had not looked at it that way before and acknowledged that there could be some truth to it. In fact, she shared this was similar feedback she received from the community she was a part of. I invited her to settle into that realization. I pointed out to her that the moment you put someone up on a pedestal, you are not only selling yourself out, but in time, you are going to want to take that person down too. It's the classic *top dog, underdog* game – one day, you will want to destroy them. You will believe that they have something you don't. That they are awakened and you are not. Waiting for the guru to tell you that you are awakened is a denial of your own awakened being. The truly awakened guru or spiritual teacher will always mirror back your always already awakened stateless state. I invited Natalie to do an exercise of self-reflection. I asked her to do a mini-life review and see how this pattern had played itself out in the last five years, to allow all the moments where she tried to *stump* the guru, except to get underneath and see her motives, and more importantly, to see what was driving her intentions. After several moments, Natalie became tearful as she was starting to see how she was denying herself. She was wanting to be mirrored and validated for her spiritual progress. With this, I invited her to not judge her experience but to sense into her already awakened nature now, independent of a teacher or the need to be seen or validated. It was important she saw the clarity of who she was now.

When we understand the self/other knot, then the dependency trap stops. Whether Natalie stayed with the community or not was irrelevant, it was important for her to drop into the depths of her being and her aloneness. I invited her to stay with her realizations and let go into the depths of the cosmic abyss with no supports, no footing whatsoever, no mirroring of any kind, or no mentoring of any kind. Natalie struggled with this, although she appeared to finally relax into it, and she was shocked how this experience or "spacelesssness" as she called it, was alive and present in the first ten years she was with the community, but she saw how they doubted it, which apparently took her out of her own realizations. The moment she desired some form of mirroring or recognition outside herself, the seed of doubt grew, which limited her to fully settle into her being. This was an explosive insight for her. We worked on this theme in several more sessions, and she began to relax her need to be seen and validated by her spiritual teacher. In fact, she commented on how she did not see any real difference between them, which allowed her to be more present and less reactive toward her guru. She was staying in her own energy of awareness more and more, and noticed less of a need to react or challenge him.

And when you come to the deepest core of your being, you will be surprised. It is what all the spiritual teachers and gurus have been pointing to all along. And maybe we will start to see the depth and truth of this in the nondual community. Perhaps the role of the guru will morph and change. Thich Nhat Hanh famously said not to be surprised if the next incarnation of Buddha is in the form of a community of love instead of a distinct being.[xlviii] You see that you don't exist as a separate person and neither does the so-called teacher, and in that seeing, there is no more question and no more answer, just an interplay of nobodies pretending to be somebodies going nowhere quickly and realizing nothing at all. The realization, then, is in the recognition that what is awake is already the case and that all apparent teachers are simply mirrors pointing you back to what is already inherently Divine and present within you, here and now. You have to die your own death. No one can do it for you.

Chapter 2: On Suffering From a Bad Case of "Zen Sickness"

An awakened life is in the recognition that existence is neither real nor unreal. It is a delicate balancing act of living the truth of emptiness while also being embodied in human form. We realize the empty nature of everything while simultaneously living the realization of our human condition. The Buddhist *Heart Sutra* captures this truth beautifully. "Form is emptiness, emptiness is form. Form is not other than emptiness; emptiness is not other than form." This Sutra illustrates what it means to live an awakened life. Life is a celebration. This realization requires a diamond like quality of awareness to cut through illusion and to avoid getting stuck in the experiences of either form or emptiness. Absolutizing one over the other happens a lot in spiritual communities, particularly with the experiences of formlessness. Many spiritual seekers get lost in emptiness, which can be a frightening and disorienting experience. There is nothing left to call a self, nothing left to call a world; there lacks any real significance to experiences, relationships, and the world at large. It has a different quality than nihilism, though. The difference being the self/other extinction. There is a real depersonalization and lack of real connection to the world. The relative world has lost all importance. It is considered a symptom of what is known as "Zen Sickness" or "emptiness sickness." It's a condition consisting of symptoms of fear, disorientation, confusion, exhaustion, "impersonalness," and hallucinatory images. But most notably, there is a deep sense of depersonalization and of being lost in emptiness.[xlix]

Awakening is such a dramatic shift away from one's usual orientation to form that there exists the very real experience of feeling lost in a limbo-like state, drifting in an endless dark vastness with nothing to hang onto. One can find themselves having difficulty relating and connecting to the world around them. Interestingly, while interviewing another participant for my master's thesis on the nondual journey towards wholeness, I met with one individual who refused to use the pronouns "I," "you," and "we," stating they don't exist and using such language gave life to separation. The world was a flat dream like state, lacking substance, meaning and significance, and any real value. During my interview with him, he often spoke of himself in the third person.

The Zen Master Han Shan reports of his experience centuries ago while leafing through a book of poems:

Imperceptibly, all the literary prose, poems and verses which I had read or written before appeared in front of me and crowded and filled space. They could not have been ejected even if my body had been nothing but open mouths, I did not even know what my body and mind were. I pondered closely over all this and felt as if my body were about to rise. I had no alternative but to let things take their course. The following day when the viceroy left, prefect Hu escorted him, and I was left alone. I thought of my experience and said to myself: 'This is exactly the Ch'an sickness that master Fa Kuang told me about.

> *Now I have caught it, and who can cure it? What I can do now is to sleep and if it is deep I will be lucky.' I then closed the door and tried to sleep. At first I could not, but a long while later I felt as if I were sleeping while seated. A boy servant knocked at the door and pushed it but received no answer. When prefect Hu returned, he learned of this and ordered that the window be broken for the studio to be entered. I was seated, wrapped in my robe. He called me but I did not answer. He shook me but I did not move.*[1]

This encounter illustrates a very real sense of depersonalization and lack of contact. It is more of a lack of understanding than narcissistic inflation. Elements of this phenomenon showed up for me in my own journey. For a few years, I did regular darkness meditations; a powerful meditation technique designed by the spiritual teacher Osho, whereby I would sit in a completely dark room and meditate with my eyes open for about an hour. There was a total absence of light. I could not see anything. Nothing at all. I would wave my hand in front of myself and see nothing at all. It was absolutely black and still. As I sat in darkness with my eyes open, I noticed thoughts would come and go and were easily followed by feelings, fears and desires, and the world of form altogether. I would allow the blackness to fill my being, and after each sitting, I would carry this darkness within my essence throughout the rest of my day. Over time, I found myself saturated in this darkness of being and was easily letting go of my worldly attachments, relaxing my hold on personal opinions and judgements, not being as reactive, and sinking further into a tranquil silence. It felt like my own unfolding of awakening was happening at an accelerated rate.

However, after several months into my practice, I started to feel a little off like I was out of balance in a way, and I was losing all interest in daily activities. Nothing seemed to matter, friends, connections, school, careers; I just didn't see what the point was anymore. I started feeling like I was in the deepest end of the ocean and lacked the interest to make contact with the people around me. There was no more reference point. Everything around me became hazy and dreamlike. I couldn't locate a self or an other, so meaning and connection gave way to a deep silence and stillness I had not experienced before. It was a silence within and without. But it wasn't a radiant emptiness, and there wasn't a full presence of being. Although I would not consider myself feeling depressed at the time, I was certainly depressing to be around. I noticed an absence of joy, humour, and emotional connectivity. I was losing a meaningful and loving way of existing in the world. I remember one instance while attending a university class in Bio-medical Ethics, where we had to submit a final paper to finish the class. Instead of writing a paper, I printed off a title page and stapled ten blank pages to be submitted. I was about to hand it in when Rob, a dear friend of mine, who was also on the nondual journey and had taken the class the previous year, suggested I use his old paper from last year and simply change it around and submit it. He sensed a disconnect within me, and looking back, I am appreciative of his compassion and quick intervention. It was around this time that a few close friends of mine shared their observations, thoughts, and feelings with me and what it was like to be in my company. Some shared feeling distant from me and having difficulty connecting, while others shared feeling a slight degree of superiority around me.

    I consulted with my friend Gary Tzu, who pointed out how I was losing connection to existence and hanging out in the void. He shared how I was becoming too attached to emptiness and setting up shop there. It's an escapist route, he said and not awakening as such. "You're hiding out in the Absolute. What good is any of that?" He said. Instead of discouraging me from continuing my darkness meditations, he suggested I alternate them with a candle meditation. He advised me to balance my meditation sessions by lighting a very small candle and placing it in the corner of the room where I meditated. It was a means of staying connected to existence and living the paradox of form and formlessness. It took a long time before I realized I had fallen into the trap of viewing the world of form as a problem or "not worth having" and isolated myself from it. There is renouncing the self and the world and living the rest of one's life in a cave, and then there is renouncing the self and the world while participating in it fully. This was key. Even though I had to ride out my experiences of depersonalization for a little while longer, I did notice a gradual return to life and a more meaningful engagement. It would take me many more years to fully appreciate, understand, and integrate these experiences in my day-to-day life.

The words found in the *Heart Sutra* – "emptiness is form, and form is emptiness" – are a reminder of the paradoxical nature of existence. The mind cannot figure it out. The moment the mind attempts to place one experience over another, division sets in and suffering ensues. Insanity exists this way. When we take one practice to be more real and everlasting against another, we lose the groundless ground of our own awakening. We are brought back into an illusion and fall under the spell of separation. When the world of form is seen as none other than formlessness, when they are seen to be one and the same, we are relaxed and wake up to our true nature of total interconnectedness. When we are really and truly empty of ourselves, emptiness becomes full of life and creativity. Life becomes a love affair. What we see and experience is inseparable from who we are. When we live in this understanding, eternity then comes into being, and life is nothing but an endless mystery.

Chapter 3: Destined for "Failurehood" and Hopelessness: Embracing the Wisdom of Defeat

Enlightenment is something which arises in you when you have utterly failed, when you have done all that you can do and there is no more to do – in that very state the let go happens.

- Osho

The mind is an achievement junkie, forever in pursuit of success, enlightenment, praise, power, and insistently climbing the ladder of human existence. It is always striving to be better than what it is now; always on the path of self-improvement and embodying a personal will to power. There is always a goal in the future which keeps the mind intact and always dominating the centre stage of life. At its root, the mind is in pursuit of leaving a personal mark on the world, having a legacy, being remembered, being immortalized in some way, and of being awakened. It is such a feverish activity. When we fall down, we're told to pick ourselves back up and keep going, to try harder. Hope is fuel for the self, hoping that one day we will succeed in life, become successful, and will finally have reached enlightenment.

If we take a sincere look within ourselves, we may be surprised to see we may have no idea why it is we are doing what we are doing. So what is driving this chase? Most of our actions are automatic and unconscious anyway. The shock is in seeing how we have been running on a never-ending treadmill, exhausting ourselves and getting nowhere. In seeing this pattern, some collapse in pure exhaustion and get off of the wheel. Here, though, instead of getting back on the wheel and hoping for a different outcome or that it will be different, perhaps we can learn to accept our defeat. This is a pivotal moment in the awakening journey. In our defeat and exhaustion, an opportunity exists. While alone and exasperated at the bottom of existence, without a clue as to what to do, the invitation is to fully accept the experience. By doing so, we become ripe for anything to happen. We are open and receiving. The mind has collapsed, and the doors of perception have opened. We are not clouded by the mind, and we are not begging for someone to come and save us; we are not reaching for our favourite nondual book to guide us, and we are totally crumpled in our own "failurehood." There is no pleading for existence to throw us a bone, and the reason is because: "Your very desire to win is going to turn into your defeat. It is the craving for success that ultimately turns into failure. Your excessive desire to live lands you in the grave. Your obsession for health is bound to turn into sickness."[li]

The desire for awakening will inevitably lead to failure. I find this particularly interesting because of how many spiritual teachers have pointed out the experience of failure and hopelessness as being a critical step in waking up out of the dream of separation. It seems that not many people want to talk about this in spiritual communities, since it doesn't sound tantalizing and hopeful. It counteracts the typical spiritual search of experiencing oneness, always being on a path, and of achieving and becoming an awakened being. And the spiritual masses may not be so inclined to pay for a workshop on embracing total "failurehood." Many people defend against this familiarity of defeatedness as it forces them to give up the spiritual identity project and the game of seeking altogether. It's nothing more than the mind trying to destroy the mind! It becomes an endless loop. Nondual teacher, John Sherman, laughed at his own predicament of trying to kill the mind:

I thought that the key to happiness was the death of the ego. So, as long as Ramana had me holding onto something that looked like ego, I was going to kill it off. Die. Die. Filled with energy, murderous energy. And I did this for weeks, months. One day I was doing it, and, in the midst of it, between one 'Die' and the next 'Die,' it just hit me. 'This thing ain't never gonna die!' And I laughed and laughed ... But the fever broke, the whole feverish insanity broke in that moment.[lii]

How can you kill something that doesn't exist? It's completely useless, and we will fail one hundred percent of the time. We are fighting amongst shadows. And there is a personal investment in spiritual seeking which keeps the sense of "I" intact. This is difficult to see, since the mind wouldn't have anything to seek anymore. It would cease running the show. When we have failed at trying to get rid of the mind, it ceases to exist. Many of us run from "failurehood" and personal defeat, however, it is just such an experience indeed that seems to have facilitated the waking up of so many beings.

There is a belief that some great nondual teachers actually woke up through a form of meditation practice or spiritual technique. For example, many scholars and spiritual seekers, alike, claim Buddha awakened by meditatively following the breath. For

Ramana Maharshi, some claim it was through deep self-inquiry, but there appears to be something fundamentally overlooked in their accounts. By looking deeper into their encounters, we can see something that points to the inherent defeat of ever achieving personal enlightenment.

It was amid their own failure at trying to be awakened that they realized the truth. For instance, returning to the story of Buddha, he left his whole family and spent several years deeply immersed in countless meditation practices, day in and day out; he devoted his entire life to the spiritual journey. He was consumed to realize who he was. He starved himself, meditated for hours, and put himself in impossible situations in order to understand his true nature and yet, nothing. It was when he became so tired and fed up at not reaching enlightenment that something happened, though. He finally stopped, and for the first time, he declared he would not move or do anything at all until the truth of his soul was revealed. There was absolutely nowhere to go. When he failed as a seeker and collapsed under the Bodhi tree, eternity was revealed, and his true nature became evident. Everything he did was met with failure, and in that space of failure and hopelessness, he awoke. The by-product of that realization was the gift of *Vipassana*, a profound meditation which he gifted to humanity.[liii]

Similarly, with the great sage Ramana Maharshi, it was the intense fear of his own inevitable death which lead to his awakening. One day, as a young teenager, while at his home, he spontaneously encountered an overwhelming sense of fear and terror at the thought of his own death and then acutely realized there was absolutely nothing he could do to prevent it. He froze in complete terror. Death was inevitable and there was absolutely no hope of overriding it. The hopelessness of his situation sparked the inner wisdom to accept the fear, terror, and hopelessness of his existential situation. It was as if he was guided by an unknown force to surrender to the experience. In doing so, grace descended and revealed the truth of who and what he was. In turn, the boon for humanity was the gift of self-inquiry.[liv] As in these accounts and many others, the experience of "failurehood" is central to waking up out of the dream of separation. Failure and hopelessness are fertile ground for spontaneous awakening to take place.

Even in our most difficult of times, such as in dealing with an illness, a job loss, or when experiencing a relationship break down, many of us are sold the gift of hope, a tranquilizing mental script, telling us it will somehow get better. We spend so much of our time and energy running away or numbing out from our incidents of failure and hopelessness, that we miss an important transformational opportunity. Hope can prolong the misery. When we accept and live the life of a walking contradiction, we are an embodiment of truth and love. Lao Tzu describes this paradox as a natural law of existence. He points out that the experience of failure is inherent to our success. They exist together, and like a pendulum, human existence moves back and forth between experiences, so to chase one end of the pendulum is to set oneself up for suffering. The invitation then, is to accept our failure and hopeless situation without judgement; to relax in the blackness of defeat and realize the underlying light of our eternal being, which is ever-present and totally untouched by the pendulating circumstances of our lives. When we relax in total surrender, we are at ease. There is no desire to win or need to be seen and appreciated, heard and admired; we saunter along in life and ride the waves of endless contradictions. When one accepts failure deep within their being, how can anyone challenge and defeat them? How can one lose when they have already accepted defeat? How can one fail if they have already embraced their own personal "failurehood?" Realizing this allows one to encounter some of life's most troubling and frightening experiences.

The Healing Power of Defeat

Once again, I draw upon my experiences with my wife dying of cancer here. After having gone through numerous rounds of chemo and radiation, experimented with various micro-biotic diets and herbal remedies, explored the benefits of dream work and meditations, and having sought out new and promising clinical trials to treat brain cancer, my wife quietly asked one evening. "It's all hopeless, isn't it?" "Yes," I replied as I held her hand. I knew it was a rhetorical question, as I could feel and sense a huge shift in her being over the last several weeks. In fact, I felt it within mine as well but did not have the heart to share it. She was letting go even further. We were both letting go. She nodded and smiled as we continued to sit in silence for some time. There was no need for an interventionist god to appear or for some type of healing miracle to happen. The mind was dissolving, and she was surrendering more and more to the process, resting in the clear spaciousness of her soul. There was a profound acceptance radiating from her. We both smiled as we lay in bed at ease with each other and completely surrendered to the fact that there was nothing we could do, nothing needed to be changed, and we could be at peace with *what is*. This was a massive realization for both of us. For her to recognize her situation was hopeless and to be able to allow that realization into her soul, was profound. She mirrored this back to me, which simultaneously allowed me to drop further into defeat, and subsequently revealed a formless state of ease. It was a beautiful descent. She seemed to give up any residual struggle and hope that things would change for the better. We both commented on how relieved we felt. After having climbed many peaks and descended into many valleys of life, our journey finally brought us both to utter failure. We gave up and settled into being with what is, recognizing and resting more and more in her true nature as the last few weeks of her life inevitably unfolded.

The thing is, though, this experience can't be reproduced, and any attempt at manufacturing it through the mind, only produces an artificial realization. There is no depth here, and one falls into the trap of pseudo awakening. Nonetheless, the mind will use this avenue as a means of self-survival; it will attempt to make failure and hopelessness into a spiritual technique and something to cultivate and work towards in time. The mind is clever and will co-opt any experience as long as it is used to support the illusion of the self. If we are open and receptive, we will notice the qualitative difference. The self co-opting the experience of failure will always feel like a clenching, whereas, when fully accepted, the true essence of failure will feel intense and explosive. It can feel like a veil has been lifted, and the essence of who we are can be felt like a vast clear valley, totally expansive and inclusive of all life, with no care in the world. There is a deep sense of ease and well-being with what arises in the moment.

In my own life and in my work counselling clients, I have found the following invitational exercise to be helpful in appreciating the inherent possibilities within the experience of failure and hopelessness. In your mind's eye, allow yourself to do a life review, from your earliest memory to this moment now in your life. See how hard you have tried to succeed at life, whether it was in your relationships, careers, school, or spiritual journey. Just notice how many times you failed miserably at trying to achieve. Notice how you have failed at being the best in your career, the best husband or wife, the best partner, the best father or mother, or the best friend. See how you have failed at being vulnerable and open, successful at spiritual seeking, and, especially, at being Awakened. See how, when you thought you had finally succeeded, failure was not far along. Notice how your life pendulates between apparent failure and success. You may be shocked to notice how you have so totally failed at even being a separate self amongst other separate selves. Allow this in and see how your efforts at trying to be or become are totally hopeless in the face of raw reality. See how reality crushes you one hundred percent of the time. See how your life trajectories are often interrupted by life itself and how you desperately try to get back on track. As you observe all of this in your life's review, notice *that* which was present all along and *that* which is here and now and untouched by it all. Notice the absolute truth of your nature, which is prior to it all.

Chapter 4: Locked in Frustration: Chasing the Illusion of a 24-Hour Ecstasy

You want something like a round-the-clock ecstasy. Ecstasies come and go, necessarily, for the human brain cannot stand the tension for a long time. A prolonged ecstasy will burn out your brain unless it is extremely pure and subtle.

- Nisargaddata Maharaj

Have you ever reached the state of seeing the "blue pearl" in your mind's eye only to see it suddenly slip away and leave you feeling utterly frustrated? Still haven't achieved a *Siddhi* type of experience to show off to your spiritual friends, and can't figure out why? Still unable to maintain that uninterrupted state of absolute tranquil calmness in your everyday life while claiming the experience of *no-self*? Are you dumbfounded that you have been meditating every day for the last decade, and wondering why the grand light show of enlightenment hasn't arrived yet? If so, it would appear you are not alone. There exists a problem of chasing enlightenment through ecstasy and bliss type experiences. There is a tendency to relegate awakening exclusively to bright lights, subtle sounds, and beautiful visionary experiences, and the ability to maintain them for a prolonged period of time, defines whether one is awakened or not. Spiritual encounters are being used as a means to define awakening. They can be so addicting and so intoxicating. There is a belief that if you're not continually riding the wave of a blissed-out experience, then you haven't tasted the divine nor have you reached enlightenment. But the desire for spiritual type experiences is nothing but unfulfilled desires that keep one locked up in a perpetual state of frustration. Although subtle and exciting, they are attachments which bind the self to the illusion of time and transcendent happenings. The lure of intense spiritual experiences can be a barrier to awakening.

In my early twenties, I was locked in this pattern during some time for many years. I remember being fascinated with reading stories and seeing pictures of all these spiritual seekers seemingly blissed out, rocking the sitar, screaming and chanting, while the guru was in a state of sublime ecstasy, appearing unfazed by it all.

This had a huge impact on me. It was so enticing and alluring. I envisioned an awake being as one having an intense gazing stare, radiating absolute sublime ecstasy in every moment, and who hardly said anything because silence was the most powerful language when it came to awakening. Their silent transmission would carry weight and be a transformative agent of enlightenment. Everything would be communicated through silence. I would spend many hours in various types of meditations as a means of dissolving into the night of awareness and triggering endless bliss and radical intensity. It all sounded wonderful, and although there were subtle clear periods of bliss and brilliancy, it never lasted long. And so, I would go back again and again and crank the wheel of effort, hoping to achieve a permanent state, which would inevitably pass. I was persistent and tried every angle, but I was always left feeling frustrated. I always returned to the same old me, the same old awkward personality; I was caught in my own misery. My preconceptions of awakening were crushed when I learned that drugs and alcohol influenced some wild displays of energetic bliss I had read about and seen in some of my favourite books and videos. Many gurus and spiritual teachers relied on drugs to induce a transcendent type of glow and hysterical laughter. I was stunned when I learned this. Like many, I felt deceived, lied to, and betrayed. How much of it was charisma and cunningness, and what reflected true enlightened *beingness*? I wondered. Even today, at workshops and conferences alike, there seems to be a manufactured type of intensity among participants, embracing bliss and passion in their transformational processes while in a group session or conference, but while at home, become shut down and are miserable. While giving *Satsang*, the spiritual teacher Papaji once asked a spiritual seeker:

"'How did you come here?' He asked.

'By train.'

'And from the station to the Ashram?'

'Where is the train now?'

I said, 'The train was at the station and now it has gone. From there I took a bullock cart to you. I sent the cart away once I got to the ashram.' Then he said, 'You made use of the train, but then you left it behind. Then you took a cart and also left it behind when you arrived to see me because it was of no further use. Like this, all the things you performed are of no use now and they will be left behind. ... What comes and goes is of no use; all your bhaktis, meditations and chanting was to direct you to some Light and now are of no use.'"[lv]

The problem was found in seeking. As a young adult, even though I had read so much about dropping the search, that seeking leads to suffering, and the importance of embracing the ordinariness of this moment, none of it registered at a deep cellular level. I may have pretended to act as though I had realized this, however, there was no grace. The error is in thinking that the mind and body will become awakened. I was seeking awakening through the body-mind, which left me in a perpetual cycle of suffering. I was seeking enlightenment through that which is temporary; I was chasing my own tail; I couldn't see the dualistic split I was living in.

Despite feeling bewildered and frustrated, my preconceptions about awakening began to break down. But then I came across this old Zen story, and something clicked:

One day a young Buddhist on his journey home came to the banks of a wide river. Staring hopelessly at the great obstacle in front of him, he pondered for hours on just how to cross such a wide barrier. Just as he was about to give up his pursuit to continue his journey he saw a great teacher on the other side of the river. The young Buddhist yells over to the teacher, 'Oh wise one, can you tell me how to get to the other side of this river?' The teacher ponders for a moment looks up and down the river and yells back, 'My son, you are on the other side.'[lvi]

I felt immobilized, like an arrow had pierced my heart. It was such a simple story, and yet I felt so incredibly impacted. For the first time, I felt like I could resonate with the young neophyte Buddhist in the story. Awakening is already the case. You, as you are, at this moment, are awakened. There is absolutely nothing you need to do. I have read this so many times in books and heard it said repeatedly during many nondual group and spiritual workshops I had attended, but now, in this moment, I felt a radical shift take place, as if something had finally sunk in. Seeking is utterly hopeless, and awakening is found in the instance of each and every moment; high and low type experiences, blissful and boring ones too. No experience, no matter how enlightening, can define awakening. It felt like my mind had thinned out and there was simply spaciousness and the clear recognition that it did not matter what presented itself in awareness, everything had a time limit in experience. Everything presented itself in the background of silence and enlightenment; feelings, insights, and ecstatic spiritual states, are all held in this vast empty awareness.

The ordinariness of this moment contains the eternal presence of who we are. It contains all time; past, present, and future. Everything exists here, in the instance of this moment. There is nothing to do, nowhere to go, nothing to say; it all just clicked simultaneously. It was all a form of seeking. Chasing spiritual highs keeps the mind active and involved. It was another self-survival strategy. Ultimate transcendence is beyond any and all experiences. Whether we are enjoying a run in the forest, a cup of coffee, shoveling snow, or sharing an embrace with a loved one, bliss is found here. Not as a powerful energetic emotion, although that may be the case, but in the thin clear spaciousness of *no-self*.

Once again, the "I" is what keeps the wheel of seeking and the desire for awakened experiences alive. See through the "I," and the desire for experiences dissolves. The "I" is what sets up the awakening game. It's all a mind game set up to keep the sense of the self alive and in control; it becomes another endless mind project of chasing and maintaining intense blissful occurrences. It gives the mind something to do; it projects itself into the future of achieving some awakened state, failing to see that awakening is already the case. The mind is so clever. This is how it stays alive and maintains a state of separateness. Without the seeking, the chase, the endless effort of holding onto bliss, the mind has nothing to do, and this is a frightening experience for the mind because with nothing to do and nowhere to go, the "I" fades out.

Awakening cannot be confined, defined, or even located in any experience. Awakening is the *suchness* of this present moment beyond all encounters. We set this whole game up for ourselves. When we become over energized with non-ordinary experiences and believe them to have lasting power, we suffer. Awakening is beyond any and all experience, but we are so easily seduced by the mind, where it is easy to find ourselves lost in a labyrinth of temporary transcendent sights, sounds, and illuminations.

When we grasp at subtle sounds and visions and use them to define who we are, we are back to betraying the essence of who we are. We are attempting to pin down that which has no name or form, and yet is found in every experience. The danger is in believing such events to represent a marker of being awake. Thinking the thought, "I am Bliss" actually takes us further away from truth. It is just a thought. We seek that which is impermanent and dramatize our frustration as if we are unworthy of our essential birthright that is an awakened being. The important question to ask ourselves is, "To whom do all these experiences occur to?" Such inquiry invites us to look within and see what is already present. In seeing this, the drive to chase spiritual encounters ceases. We are no longer deceived by the mind and tricked into believing such experiences will lead to or even produce an enlightened experience. A spiritual encounter will never tell you who and what you are. Truth is always present prior to that, during, and after any type of experience. The recognition is in seeing that the transformational energy is not in any type of experience, but rather, is in the clear spacious moment from which all experiences arise and subside.

One night, I connected with a dear friend of mine, Kaitlyn, and we had a wonderful discussion about the experience of boredom and the transformational power it held. For her, the lust for intense white-light encounters was beginning to fade out. She recently attended a nondual therapy group and was finding all the nondual talk and ecstatic experiences everyone was having to be quite boring and repetitive. She shared how she expressed her thoughts and feelings and observations to the group. While expecting to be verbally attacked and judged by the group, she was surprised to find the facilitator inviting her and the rest of the group to sit in the feelings of boredom and to celebrate it. Kaitlyn smiled, describing how blissful and relaxing it was to simply be bored and to share her familiarity of it with the rest of the group. Her mind slowed down, the mental commentary about what she was observing and concluding within the group subsided, and she sat in the heart of boredom. "Who knew boredom could be such a spiritual experience?" She shared. Interestingly, she recalled believing, "If I wasn't blissed out, that meant I wasn't awake." I could resonate with her experiences. The mind turned boredom into a pathology and sought escape from it. The mind seeks refuge in an experience; it seeks sanctuary in time, in the past and future. But within the moment is where it dissolves. This moment, no matter what is happening, this is the most spiritual experience we could be having.

Letting go of the illusion of a twenty-four-hour ecstasy is an important part of the awakening journey. We need to relax our tendencies of being self-mesmerized by our own illusions. Relax at this moment and see that nothing matters, nothing at all. The miracle isn't in performing spiritual healing; the miracle is realizing you are already awake. We wake up from the lust and desire of spiritual experiences. We see that they are there to mirror back to us the need to let go even further. They arise to remind us "this isn't it." They are enjoyed and celebrated in the moment, yet are entirely let go of all the same. Be anchored in spaciousness, which contains all experiences. Be here, now, in the clear *suchness* of the moment. This is love, this is truth, and with an open hand, we live our lives. See that whatever is happening now is the most spiritual experience.

Epilogue: Just a Wandering Cosmic Nobody

Clear-eyed and imperturbable, walk through life, as though you didn't exist

- Chuang Tzu

And so, here we are, back home; back to where we all started, having never left, yet having travelled a million miles. Having abandoned it all, we found everything. Having left, we finally arrived. *This* is it and *this* has always been it. It has always been so. Just *this* moment. Just here and now. It's so ordinary, so absolutely ordinary and available. There was never anywhere to go, yet there were so many places to visit, so many experiences to share and talk about. And there was never any experience to be had, still, we are richer for having experienced so many. There were never any depths to descend to nor any heights to climb, yet the journey could not have been otherwise. And there was no one to meet, still, we met so many beautiful souls and danced the mysteries of existence. We never moved an inch, we never even took a step, we never even stepped out of the front door, and yet we journeyed the galaxy and flew through the cosmos of our being. While having never moved, we realized *this and that* collapse into themselves, revealing the brilliancy of *eternal being*. The instance we stop looking into the future or into the past to define ourselves, is the instant we arrive at ever present awareness. Just here. And that ever present stillness is so still it's louder than thunder, it's so absent we can see it everywhere and within everything imaginable. Beyond form, it nevertheless exists as form. The road of a million miles begins and ends with the first step. And our travelling companions were none other than the expressions of ourselves; all of them – beautiful, loving, fearful, and demonic; judging, accepting, friendly, and hateful; they all played their role in guiding us home, pointing us back to where we had always been, back to where we already are but seemingly having forgotten. In a deep slumber of ignorance and illusion, we believed ourselves into existence and danced the dance of separateness for millions of lives and with millions of partners; forever learning a new dance routine and endlessly changing partners, until the song abruptly ends and we are shocked out of our slumber and hear our own tune for the very first time – our original tune. We finally see that what we had been seeking to discover all this time was already available and present now. The game of hide-and-seek is now over.

There is no sense of having arrived because we had never left, and there is no sense of becoming because *this* never changes. We have arrived through non-arrival and journeyed through the land of self-discovery without having taken the first step. *This* appears as the endless display of manifestation while never losing its original shapeless shape. It exists through non-existence, and we come to realize it through unknowing by unlearning everything we come to know and experience the truth. By taking the first step, we move light years away from *this*, and yet without this error in step, we would have never experienced *this*. Seeking is a movement towards failure, and there can't be enough failure; failure brings us back to *this,* again and again, and again. Seeking truth will evidently lead to failure, the failure of finding what you already are. The failure of being a self brings us back to truth. *This* can't be added to or taken away. It can't become any more than what it already is. The mind can't catch it, describe it, understand it, know it, see it, hear it, achieve it, find it, lose it, or locate it. One can only be *It*.

This is closer than one's own breath and hides in plain sight, that's why it's difficult to see. The mind loves a challenge and will project a long and arduous search for that which is already the case. That is its mission and its sole sustenance. Seeking is food for the mind. It's the ultimate mountain to climb; the Mount Everest of human consciousness, and the mind loves a challenge. But again, none of this could have gone any other way. What more can be said? Well, maybe just *this* and *that*. As the darkness of the separate self is seen through, the moon of awakening is revealed, and we are nothing but a wandering cosmic nobody.

In a cold night, in a cold winter night, a dark night, a bird enters into a palace by one window, flutters in the room for a while – the coziness of the room, the king's palace, the light, the warmth – and then is again out of the room by another window. Buddha says so is life's dream – just a moment's warmth, a moment's coziness, a moment's palace and the pleasures of it, and again we plunge into nothingness. From nothingness we come and to nothingness we move ... and just in the middle a momentary dream.

- Osho

References

i Kherdian, D. (2004). *The Buddha: The story of an awakened life.* White Cloud Press. Ashland, Oregon.

ii Wachowski, L. and L. (Directors). (1999). *The Matrix.* Warner Bros.

iii Balsekar, R. (1998). *Your Head in the Tiger's Mouth: Talks in Bombay with Ramesh S. Balsekar.* Advaita Press. Redondo Beach, California. p. 51.

iv Osho. (1997). *Hsin Hsin Ming: The Book of Nothing: Discourses on Sosan's Verses on the Faith-Mind.* Rebel Publishing House. Pune, India. p. 1.

v Da Free John. (1978). *The Enlightenment of the whole body: A rational and new prophetic revelation of the truth of religion, esoteric spirituality, and the divine destiny of man.* Dawn Horse Press. Middleton, California. p. 564.

vi Boland, Y. (2016). *Moonology: Working with the magic of lunar cycles.* Hay House, Inc. Carlsbad, California.

vii Bradshaw, J. (1998). *Healing the shame that binds you.* Health Communications, Inc. Boca Raton, Florida.

viii Almaas, A. H. (1996). *The point of existence: Transformations of narcissism in self-realization.* Diamond Books. Berkeley, California. p. 334

ix Wilber, K. (1998). *The eye of spirit. An integral vision for a world gone slightly mad.* Shambhala. Boston, Massachusetts.

x Nirmala. (2001). *Nothing personal: Seeing beyond the illusion of a separate self.* Endless Satsang Press. Prescott, Arizona. pp. 50-51

xi Hopkins, J. (1992). *The Lizard King: The essential Jim Morrison.* Scribner Publishing. New York, New York.

xii Carnes, P. (1993). *Out of the shadows: Understanding sexual addiction.* Hazeldon Publishing. Center City, Minnesota. p. 184

xiii Almaas, A. H. (1996). *The point of existence: Transformations of narcissism in self-realization.* Diamond Books. Berkeley, California.

xiv Almaas, A. H. (1996). *The point of existence: Transformations of narcissism in self-realization.* Diamond Books. Berkeley, California. pp. 303-304.

xv Almaas, A. H. (1996). *The point of existence: Transformations of narcissism in self-realization.* Diamond Books. Berkeley, California. pp. 303-304. p. 319.

xvi Almaas, A. H. (1996). *The point of existence: Transformations of narcissism in self-realization.* Diamond Books. Berkeley, California. pp. 338.

xvii Firman, J. & Gila, A. (1997). *The primal wound: A transpersonal view of trauma, addiction, and growth.* State University of New York Press, New York, New York.

xviii Foster, J. (2009). *An extraordinary absence: Liberation in the midst of a very ordinary life.* Non-Duality Press. Salisbury, United Kingdom. p. 34.

xix Tolle, E. (1999). *The power of now: A guide to spiritual enlightenment.* New World Publishing. San Francisco, California. pp. 1-2.

xx Katie, B. (2002). *Loving what is: Four questions that can change your life.* Harmony. New York, New York. p. xii.

xxi Gangaji. (2005). *The diamond in your pocket: Discovering your true radiance.* Sounds True, Inc. Boulder, Colorado. p. 175.

xxii Renz, K. (2005). *The myth of Enlightenment: Seeing through the illusion of separation.* Inner Directions Foundation. Carlsbad, California. p. xxi.

xxiii Theriault, B. (2005). *The non-dual experience: A phenomenological hermeneutic investigation of the seeker's journey towards wholeness* [unpublished master's thesis]. The University of Lethbridge. p. 102.

xxiv Theriault, B. (2005). *The non-dual experience: A phenomenological hermeneutic investigation of the seeker's journey towards wholeness* [unpublished master's thesis]. The University of Lethbridge. p. 104.

xxv Beattie, M. (1987). *Codependent no more: How to stop controlling others and start caring for yourself.* Hazeldon Press. Center City, Minnesota.

xxvi Bonder, S. (1998). *Waking down: Beyond hypermasculine Dharmas: A breakthrough way of self-realization in the sanctuary of mutuality.* Mt. Tam Awakenings. San Rafael, California.

xxvii Chopra, S. (2008). *Yogic secrets of the dark Goddess: Lighting dance of the supreme shakti.* Wisdom Tree Publishing. New Delhi, India. p. xiii.

xxviii Castaneda, C. (1985). *The fire from within.* Pocket Books Publishing. New York, New York.

xxix Mitchell, S. (1991). *Tao Te Ching: A new English version.* Harper Perennial. New York, New York.

xxx Castaneda, C. (1985). *The fire from within.* Pocket Books Publishing. New York, New York. p. 24.

xxxi Castaneda, C. (1985). *The fire from within.* Pocket Books Publishing. New York, New York.

xxxii Weatherby, K. (2010). *Rising from Bethany: The story of Lazarus.* Tate Publishing & Enterprises. Mustang, Oklahoma.

xxxiii Osho. (1975). *Tao: The Three treasures: Volume 1.* Rajneesh Foundation Ltd. Poona, India. pp. 32-33.

xxxiv Osho. (1984). *No water, no moon: Talks on Zen stories.* Rajneesh Foundation International. Rajneeshpuram, Oregon.

xxxv Osho. (1979). *Zen: The path of paradox: Volume 3.* Rajneesh Foundation Ltd. Poona, India.

xxxvi Wolinsky, S. *Notes from the dream: Circa 1982-1986.* Quantum Institute Press. (2011). pp. 55-56. http://stephenhwolinskyphdlibrary.com

xxxvii Adyashanti. (2010). *The end of your world: Uncensored straight talk on the nature of Enlightenment.* Sounds True, Inc. Boulder, Colorado. p. 209.

xxxviii Lyne, A. (Director). (1990). *Jacob's Ladder.* Carolco Pictures.

xxxix Adi Da. (1991). *Easy death: Spiritual discourses and essays on the inherent and ultimate transcendence of death and everything else* (2nd Edition). The Dawn Horse Press. Clearlake, California. pp. 147-148.

xl Osho. (1994). *Heartbeat of the absolute: Commentaries on the Ishavasya Upanishad*. Element Books Ltd. Dorset, United Kingdom. pp. 131-132.

xli Pillay, K. (1996). *Death and the transcendence of grief.* Noumenon: A Newsletter for the Nondual Perspective. Retrieved from http://www.noumenon.co.za/html/autumn_1996.html_para.8.

xlii Greenspan, M. (2003). *Healing through the dark emotions. The wisdom of grief, fear, and despair.* Shambhala. Boston, Massachusetts. pp. 90-91.

xliii Bedard, J. (1999). Lotus in the fire: The healing power of Zen. Shambhala. Boston, Massachusetts. pp. 112-113.

xliv Tolle, E. (1999). *The power of now: A guide to spiritual Enlightenment.* New World Publishing. San Francisco, California.

xlv Theriault, B. (2005). *The non-dual experience: A phenomenological hermeneutic investigation of the seeker's journey towards wholeness* [unpublished master's thesis]. The University of Lethbridge. p. 145.

xlvi Sasaki, S. (2010). *The story of the giant disciples of Buddha: Ananda and Maha-Kasyapa.* Kessinger Publishing. Whitefish, Montana.

xlvii Osho. (1999). *The diamond sutra: Discourses on the vajrachchedika prajnaparamita sutra of Guatama the Buddha* (2nd Edition). The Rebel Publishing House. Pune India. p. 121.

xlviii Thich Nhat Hanh (1994). The next Buddha may be a sangha. *Inquiring Mind*. 10(2). https://www.inquiringmind.com/article/1002_41_thich-nhat_hanh/

xlix Waddell, N. (2010). *Wild ivy: The spiritual autobiography of Zen master Hakuin*. Shambhala. Boulder, Colorado.

l Luk, C. (1971). *Practical Buddhism*. Rider Publishing. London, United Kingdom. pp. 84-85.

li Osho. (2002). *Krishna: The man and his philosophy* (5th Edition). Jaico Publishing House. Mumbai, India. p. 271.

lii Sherman, J. (2010). *Look at yourself.* SilentHeart Press/ RiverGanga Foundation. Ojai, California. pp. 63-64.

liii Kherdian, D. (2004). *The Buddha: The story of an awakened life.* White Cloud Press. Ashland, Oregon.

liv Osborne, A. (2001). *For those with little dust: Pointers on the teachings of Ramana Maharshi* (2nd Edition). Inner Directions Publishing.

lv Poonja, H. W. L. (2000). *The truth is.* Samuel Weiser, Inc. York Beach, Maine. p. 434.

lvi Craig, T. (2014, April 18). *The other side*. Tao of a Zen warrior. https://zenrevolution.wordpress.com/2014/04/18/the-other-side/

CPSIA information can be obtained
at www.ICGtesting.com
Printed in the USA
BVHW030202160422
634500BV00006B/74